250 Anecdotes About Opera

David Bruce

Published by David Bruce, 2022.

While every precaution has been taken in the preparation of this book, the publisher assumes no responsibility for errors or omissions, or for damages resulting from the use of the information contained herein.

250 ANECDOTES ABOUT OPERA

First edition. August 3, 2022.

Copyright © 2022 David Bruce.

ISBN: 979-8201330293

Written by David Bruce.

Table of Contents

Dedication

Dedicated to My Sister Brenda

Brenda wrote, "During COVID and when visitors were restricted from visiting their loved one in the assisted-living facility I worked at, a patient mentioned to me how much she liked spaghetti during a late-night conversation we had. She was a night owl like me. Her name was Dee. I called her "Gerdy." Then she would say, "Dirty Gerdy," and we'd laugh. Anyway, on my way to work I bought two spaghetti meals from Olive Garden. I left for work early that night. I went to work, set up outlet dinners in the dining room, went to her room and wheeled her down to the dining room where we had dinner together. At that time, the residents weren't leaving their room and had their meals alone in their room. It was nighttime and everyone was already in bed, so I didn't see a problem. She was so grateful and had enough food for three more meals. It was such a simple gesture, but during that time it meant so much to her and for me."

Brenda once bought a newspaper at a gas station on Thanksgiving and tipped the female employee $5, and the employee cried.

Brenda wrote, "I do remember that. I also remember when George tipped a TeeJays waitress $100, and she cried. Our family does a lot of good deeds all the time: I unload people's grocery carts when the people are in those electric scooters. If they are alone with a few groceries, I'll leave cash for the cashier to pay for the groceries. I've had a lot of good deeds done to me when I didn't have a lot of money. It feels good to pay it forward."

She added, "I just have one more thing to add and then I'm done. I've had a lot of people in my life do good deeds for me when I was at a low point on my life. I was at a low point for a very long time. David, you know what you've done for me, and I can never thank you enough. Martha paid for antibiotics for me when I had strep throat and didn't have money. Rosa bought me groceries. Carla has done so much, and she had us over for Easter just after Chad died. When I say US, I mean all of my kids. She was so sick and ended up at the Emergency Room that same night. Frank gave me a car. And George buys my gas for me whenever he's in Florida. And Mom and Dad were good people. I had a lot of good influences in my life that made me be a good person. At least I hope I'm a good person. I try to be someone Mom and Dad would be proud of."

***

The doing of good deeds is important. As a free person, you can choose to live your life as a good person or as a bad person. To be a good person, do good deeds. To be a bad person, do bad deeds. If you do good deeds, you will become good. If you do bad deeds, you will become bad. To become the person you want to be, act as if you already are that kind of person. Each of us chooses what kind of person we will become. To become a good person, do the things a good person does. To become a bad person, do the things a bad person does. The opportunity to take action to become the kind of person you want to be is yours.

Front Cover Photograph for *250 Anecdotes About Opera*:
https://pixabay.com/photos/land-mark-opera-house-sydney-night-3417124/

Chapter 1: From Advertisements to Children

Advertisements

• For a while, Pierre Monteux conducted for Serge Diaghilev and his ballet troupe, resulting in a reputation of being a ballet rather than an opera conductor, despite the vast number of operas he had conducted. When Mr. Monteux began conducting for the Metropolitan Opera House, the New York critics made this criticism of him, and a leading arts magazine especially made this criticism of him, but Otto Kahn told him, "Don't worry, Monteux. I will take care of this." Mr. Monteux wondered how Mr. Kahn could stop the criticism, but Mr. Kahn easily solved the problem. He simply paid $500 for an advertisement for Mr. Monteux in the leading arts magazine, and the criticism magically stopped.[1]

• Giuseppe di Stefano had pride. In Philadelphia, Pennsylvania, he once announced that he would not sing a concert because he had discovered that the concert programs contained an advertisement for "the world's greatest opera singer, Franco Corelli." Mr. di Stefano did sing the concert — but only after the programs had been taken away from the audience and placed in his dressing room.[2]

Advice

• Opera singer Lillian Nordica was shocked by a young woman who had been singing with an opera company in England. Ms. Nordica wanted her to audition for the Metropolitan Opera, where she was sure the young singer could get the role of a Page in *Romeo and Juliet*. However, the young singer replied, "Oh, I wouldn't sing a secondary role." Ms. Nordica felt that the singer was making "a great mistake. To sing well one beautiful aria on the same stage with such artists as the two De Reszkes and Madame Melba would do her more good than to sing the first roles in a poor company."[3]

• Theater director Tyrone Guthrie was a fan of opera — and also of Verdi's *Requiem*. Often, he would sing along with his recording and shout, "Yes! Yes!" His wife, Judy, occasionally asked him, "Tony, can we just listen to it?" Mr. Guthrie always replied by shouting, "No — get involved!"[4]

Age

• At the age of 93, Mary Garden's mother died, but at the age of 35, she stopped counting how many years she had lived. She once told her daughter, "Mary, I was never 36 and I never shall be." The two sometimes traveled together, but Mary was sometimes embarrassed because according to her mother's passport, her mother was one year old when she gave birth to her.[5]

• Cosima Wagner, Richard's wife and then widow, had a remarkable intelligence, even in her old age. Conductor Karl Muck once argued with her about a passage by a philosopher. Afterward, he went to bed at his hotel, but he was woken by Cosima, who was throwing stones at his window. He went to the window, and Cosima yelled up at him, "I've got the book here. Come down. I am right!"[6]

• When Mabel Wagnalls interviewed Lilli Lehmann, she was shocked when Ms. Lehmann mentioned her date of birth, so she said, "The American ladies so seldom give their age that your frankness is a revelation." Ms. Lehmann smiled, then replied, "Why not? One is thereby no younger."[7]

Alcohol

• Opera singer Clara Doria once was seasick during a voyage and was unable to eat, but the wife of a clergyman declared that she was suffering from starvation, not from seasickness. The clergyman's wife recommended that she drink a gin cocktail with Angostura bitters, and when Ms. Doria did, her appetite immediately returned and her seasickness vanished. Ms. Doria told this story to her friends, and when she left on another sea voyage, many of her friends got her quart bottles of gin cocktail as a farewell gift. Some of her friends went separately to a man named Billy Pitcher to buy quarts of gin cocktail, telling him that they were gifts for Ms. Doria, and he was amazed and asked, "Good Lord, what sort of woman is Ms. Doria? Does she drink cocktail by the gallon, or does she take a bath in it?"[8]

• Opera singer Kirsten Flagstad enjoyed drinking, but she didn't like to drink before noon. Therefore, she and her accompanist, Edwin McArthur, would sit and watch the clock slowly move its hands toward noon. However, during one of their train trips from New York to San Francisco, Mr. McArthur occasionally would get tired of waiting, so he would say, "Oh, for heaven's sake, in New York it's already nearly two — we can start." Then he would pour two glasses.[9]

• The great tenor Enrico Caruso occasionally took a drink during the rigors of recording opera. He once disappeared for a few minutes while recording a duet from *Madame Butterfly* with Geraldine Farrar. When he returned and they started recording again, Ms. Farrar mischievously added these words to her part of the duet, "Oh, you've had a highball!" Mr. Caruso in turn sang these words: "No, I've had two highballs." The recording is now a collector's item.[10]

• During a 1964 performance of *The Magic Flute* at the Glyndebourne Festival, two free-standing triangular pillars (and the stagehands inside them) on stage toppled and fell to the floor. The performers on stage, Heinz Blankenburg and Ragnar Ulfung, looked at each other, then walked backstage and righted the pillars, all the while ad-libbing in German about how effectively Guinness (an alcoholic beverage) builds strength. The audience cheered.[11]

• Soprano Giulia Grisi (1811-1869) strongly believed in the restorative power of beer. While performing in Donizetti's *Lucrezia Borgia*, she was required to fall on the stage and lie there, so she arranged for a glass of beer to be handed to her through a trapdoor in the floor of the stage. With her back to the audience and the glass hidden from the audience's sight, she guzzled the beer to gain strength to continue her performance.[12]

Animals

• Ivan Jadan, the premier lyric tenor of the Bolshoi Opera from 1928-1941, lived in the Virgin Islands for the last part of his life. He swam nearly every day, and in 1957 he made a friend of a black angelfish with five gold bands. Often, he crushed a sea egg and fed it to the angelfish. One day, he discovered the angelfish in an old, abandoned fish trap. Mr. Jadan knew that the angelfish would die if it stayed there, so he crushed a sea egg in his hand, then put his hand into the trap's intricate opening. The angelfish swam to the food, Mr. Jadan moved his hand away, and the angelfish followed the hand and food to freedom. Mr. Jadan didn't name the angelfish until 1993, when he told his great-niece Anna about the pretty little angelfish and announced that its name was Anna Angelfish.[13]

• Nineteenth-century impresario Colonel James H. Mapleson once needed tenor Luigi Ravelli to sing in *Carmen*, but Mr. Ravelli sent him word shortly before the opera began — much too late to change the opera — that he could not sing that night. Arriving at Mr. Ravelli's hotel, Colonel Mapleson was surprised to see that Mr. Ravelli appeared to be in good health, even though he was in bed. He tested Mr. Ravelli's voice at the piano, and discovered that Mr. Ravelli was in good voice. It appeared that Mr. Ravelli would sing that night after all, but unfortunately, Mr. Ravelli placed great trust in his favorite dog, Niagara. He asked the dog if he should sing, the dog growled, and Mr. Ravelli went back to bed.[14]

• Soprano Geraldine Farrar once held a live goose while taking a curtain call after a performance in Engelbert Humperdinck's *Die Koenigskinder*. The goose honked, and the audience applauded. Tenor Leo Slezak noticed all the attention Ms. Farrar was getting, so he said that he would carry a swan with him for his curtain call after his next performance of *Lohengrin*. "Go ahead," she said, laughing, "but you can pinch your swan all you want — he won't squawk because he is stuffed."[15]

• Maria Jeritza appeared with Enrico Caruso in *Carmen*. Often animals are used in the production of operas, and often the animals are not house broken. A horse once befouled — and befouled — the stage during a performance, and when the climatic moment came when Mr. Caruso "stabbed" Ms. Jeritza, she refused to die. Under his breath, a shocked Mr. Caruso said, "Die! Fall, will you?" Ms. Jeritza whispered back, "I'll die if you can find me a clean place."[16]

• Sir Peter Ustinov introduced his young daughter to opera by way of a performance of *Aida*. Unfortunately, late in the opera, several animals (including horses, camels, and elephants) began to relieve themselves on stage. Mr. Ustinov's daughter — a polite young lady — tapped his shoulder and asked, "Daddy, is it all right if I laugh?"[17]

• Animals are occasionally used onstage during operas. Once, Sir Thomas Beecham was conducting the Triumphal Scene from Verdi's *Aida* when a horse relieved itself on stage. Sir Thomas told the audience, "A distressing spectacle, ladies and gentlemen, but what a critic!"[18]

• Franco Corelli's dog was well trained. While Mr. Corelli was on stage singing, his dog was in Mr. Corelli's dressing room. If anyone entered the dressing room and reached for Mr. Corelli's paycheck, the dog bit him.[19]

Audiences

• Geraldine Farrar and Enrico Caruso once performed together in the opera *Carmen*. Ms. Farrar had recently acted in a movie version of *Carmen*, and she incorporated a bit of business from the movie into the onstage opera — she slapped Mr. Caruso with her fan — not hard enough to hurt him — in the last act. Mr. Caruso was a good sport, and during the curtain call he rubbed his cheek as if he had been hurt. He had not been hurt, of course, but was merely joking. However, members of the audience were convinced that Ms. Farrar had really hit Mr. Caruso hard, and reporters were soon asking Ms. Farrar why she had struck Mr. Caruso. She knew that the reporters wanted a good story, and she gave them a good story — she denied nothing. Soon, Mr. Caruso called Mr. Farrar and said, "What is this? The reporters — the many reporters — say I am very angry because you slap. I not like. I worry." Ms. Farrar told him, "Stop worrying. Deny nothing. Do you know what's going to happen? Next week, when you and I repeat *Carmen*, everybody will want to see whether I slap you hard again. The house will be packed." Ms. Farrar remembered later, "That's just the way it was. The next week Enrico and I did *Carmen* again. The house was packed."[20]

• Early in his career, American-born tenor Richard Tucker had to grow used to the customs of other countries. In Verona, Italy, he started to sing softly at a rehearsal, not aware that in Verona many people come to rehearsals. As he sang softly, he heard a commotion from the audience, and conductor Tullio Serafin explained that the people in the audience had not heard his records, which were not then available in Italy, and so they were wondering whether he could sing. Mr. Tucker then sang full voice, and the audience stormed the stage and kissed him. At the actual performance of the opera, Mr. Tucker did not know that audience members light candles to show their appreciation of exceptionally well-sung arias. Therefore, he was astonished to suddenly see hundreds of candles being lit in front of him. At the conclusion of the aria, the audience starting shouting, "*Bis*! *Bis*!" ("*Bis*!" means "Twice!" or "Encore!") He thought the audience was shouting "Beast!" at him. After the opera, he asked his wife, "Sara, what happened?" She explained to him that he had scored another huge success.[21]

• Early in the history of opera, candles lit the theaters. Members of the audience bought librettos, which indicated when favorite arias would be sung, to read during performances. Frequently, instead of waiting for a favorite aria, members of the audience would go out for a bite to eat, then return later, in time for the aria — or they would visit with other members of the audience as they waited. It wasn't until the invention of the electric light that theaters became dark — and audiences became silent. In fact, early in the history of operas, the overture was written to alert the chattering audience that the performance was about to begin — Wolfgang Amadeus Mozart and Gioacchino Rossini often wrote overtures that began with a few loud chords to get the audience's attention.[22]

• Critic Erica Jeal saw the famous Three Tenors in concert at Wembley Stadium on July 6, 1996, but she did run into a problem: "The gentleman in the seat behind me found, to his delight and my despair, that he could sing along to half of the numbers." This was especially a problem because listening to a concert of the Three Tenors — Luciano Pavarotti, Plácido Domingo, and José Carreras — was very expensive although the Three Tenors concerts had a reputation of bringing opera to a non-elitist and non-exclusive audience. Ms. Jeal says pointedly, "For the price of my press ticket for Wembley [a British sports stadium] I could have seen at least 40 performances at the Coliseum [British opera house] — who's being exclusive now?"[23]

• Hans Hotter made his operatic debut in Vienna, Austria, in the role of Jochanaan in *Salome*. After the debut, his mother, who had been present, overheard two teenagers — a male and a female — who had separately seen him perform and who were talking about him. The girl said, "Have you heard that man — the naked one [Jochanaan's costume was only a camel skin] with the huge voice?" The boy replied, "I don't know about the voice, but did you see those great arms which he stretched out when he was pronouncing the curse? My word, he would be the right member for our Danube rowing club!"[24]

• Carlo Bergonzi, following the wishes of Giuseppe Verdi, sang softly the final B flat of "*Celeste Aida*" at the Teatro Regio, Parma, in December 1959. Unfortunately, the audience was displeased, not being used to hearing that note sung softly. After the opera, an audience member approached Mr. Bergonzi to ask why he had varied from tradition. Of course, Mr. Bergonzi explained that Verdi had written the note that way. Unfortunately, the audience member was still not satisfied, remarking, "So Verdi was wrong, too!"[25]

• Audiences have various ways of showing disapproval. In Mexico, during a very poor performance of the opera *Trovatore*, a tenor mangled "*Di quella pira.*" Following the song, the audience did not applaud, but instead made the sound "SHH!" In 1969, at a performance of *Rigoletto* in Edinburgh, Scotland, the singer playing the Duke of Mantua mangled "*Parmi veder le lagrime.*" Following the song, the audience showed its displeasure by remaining absolutely silent and absolutely still.[26]

• At the end of the Second World War, Galiano Masini was performing as Cavaradossi in *Tosca* at the Teatro Verdi. Unfortunately, he struggled vocally for the first two acts, and the audience loudly and persistently criticized him. However, Mr. Masini performed a marvelous "*E' lucevan le stelle*" in the final act, and the audience reversed itself and shouted for an encore. Mr. Masini strode to the footlights, glared at the audience, and then told them (presumably in Italian), "Up yours!"[27]

• Baritone Antonio Tamburini was a versatile singer. During the carnival season in Palermo in 1822, the audience came armed with noise-makers such as drums and trumpets. The prima donna was frightened by the loudness and rowdiness of the crowd, so Mr. Tamburini performed and sang both his part and her part — for the duets, he sang his part with his normal baritone and he sang her part with a falsetto. The audience loved it.[28]

• In the old opera house, members of the Metropolitan Opera Guild gathered in a box. A rule of silence was imposed in the box during performances, but the rule was ignored in the case of Guild member and retired Met tenor Giovanni Martinelli. While attending the opera, Mr. Martinelli was accustomed to hum throughout the performance — and occasionally to criticize it.[29]

• Jean de Reszke sacrificed for his art. For example, while appearing as Siegfried to Nellie Melba's Brünnhilde (her sole appearance in that role), he sacrificed his mustache. However, his fans were outraged by its non-appearance, and Mr. de Reszke restored it when he sang Siegfried in London in future appearances.[30]

Auditions

• A lucky break helped soprano Leslie Garrett get a job with the English National Opera. She was singing the part of Susanna in *The Marriage of Figaro* when she received word that English National Opera managing director Lord Harewood would be present at a performance. Normally, Ms. Garrett paced herself so that she could get through all four acts. However, since Lord Harewood would be present, she decided to sing all-out from the very beginning and trust that some extra strength would providentially arrive to help her get through the end of the opera. She did sing all out from the very beginning, performing brilliantly in the first two acts, but unfortunately extra strength did not arrive, so she sang poorly in the last two acts. She thought that she blown her chances of ever singing in the English National Opera, but luck was with her. Lord Harewood had left after the first two acts, and shortly afterward she got a job singing with the English National Opera.[31]

• Throughout her career, soprano Helen Traubel was compared to another great soprano: Kirsten Flagstad. Early in her career, Ms. Traubel auditioned for a radio program, although she had broken out in fiery spots because of an allergy to a kitten she had cuddled. In the middle of the audition, she noticed the radio engineers in the control room laughing, and she assumed that they were laughing at her appearance, so she threatened to leave. However, they convinced her to stay, explaining that they were laughing because the radio bigwigs, who were listening in an upstairs room, had called to tell them, "Stop your kidding. Turn off that Flagstad record and let that kid you're going to audition start singing."[32]

• Soprano Beverly Sills felt that she was too tall to sing the title role in *The Ballad of Baby Doe*, but eventually she agreed to audition for the role. She wore high spiked heels that made her even taller, and before she began to sing, she said, "This is how big I am before I sing, and I'm going to be just as big when I finish. So if I'm too big for your Baby Doe, you can save my energy and your time by saying so right now." The composer of the opera, Douglas Moore, told her she looked "just fine," and after she had sung, he was awed and told her, "Oh, Miss Sills, you are Baby Doe."[33]

• In June of 1897, Enrico Caruso, then an unknown, auditioned for Giacomo Puccini and made an immediate impact. After Mr. Caruso had sung "*Che gelida manina*," Mr. Puccini turned from the piano he was playing as accompaniment, looked at Mr. Caruso, and asked, "Who has sent you to me — God?"[34]

Autographs

• American soprano Grace Moore became famous in opera, musical comedy, and movies — in opera, she is best known for her Louise, which she studied under Gustave Charpentier. One day, Garbo visited her and her husband at their house in Connecticut in response to an invitation to stay for the weekend. Before Sunday lunch, Ms. Moore asked Garbo and her other guests to sign their names in her guest-book. Garbo disliked giving autographs, so she declined to sign the guest-book. Ms. Moore told her, "If my house is not good enough for you to let others know you have been here, I think you had better leave immediately. I shall have the car ready to take you back to New York in 15 minutes." Within 15 minutes, Garbo was in the car and headed for New York.[35]

• Following a recital in Boston, Massachusetts, by soprano Marilyn Horne, a woman with a seeing-eye dog asked Ms. Horne to autograph her program. First, however, Ms. Horne asked about the seeing-eye dog and whether she could pat him. The blind woman replied, "It's a her. Her name is Gloria, and sure, you can pat her." Ms. Horne patted

Gloria, and then she signed the program. A little later, the blind woman and a friend came back, and the friend asked Ms. Horne to re-sign the program. Ms. Horne looked at the program and saw that she had written, "Dear Gloria, Many thanks for being with me today. Sincerely, Marilyn Horne." Ms. Horne commented, "It may be the only time a dog has received an autograph."[36]

Automobiles

• Basso Ferruccio Furianetto took care of his voice over the years, turning down roles that he felt his voice was not ready for. Conductor Herbert von Karajan once asked him to sing the role of Escamillo, which is a role for a baritone. Immediately, Mr. Furianetto changed the subject to something that he knew Mr. Karajan would want to talk about: "Maestro, did you see the new Porsche that just came out?" Later, Mr. Furianetto said, "That Porsche saved me!"[37]

• When Pierre Monteux started working at the Metropolitan Opera, he decided to buy a shiny Ford touring-car. He paid $300 for the car, which he was proud of at first, although it looked modest when parked beside the luxurious cars of the stars of the Met. However, the car did give Mr. Monteux trouble. One day, as he was driving it, the car developed engine trouble and stopped. Mr. Monteux got out of the car, tipped his hat to it, and walked away, never to return.[38]

Ballet

• Adam Pernell once provided piano accompaniment for David Howard's class when Rudolf Nureyev was taking it. Mr. Pernell was feeling depressed, so he started playing music that was appropriate to his mood — the death scene of Violetta in *La Traviata*. Mr. Nureyev danced the appropriate steps, but as he danced he mimed Violetta's consumptive cough. From that beginning, a game developed between Mr. Pernell and Mr. Nureyev. Mr. Pernell would play music from an opera, and Mr. Nureyev would dance the steps as the character from the opera would dance them. Each time, Mr. Nureyev got the opera and the character right. Afterwards, Mr. Pernell left class in a wonderful mood.[39]

• Richard Wagner brought his opera *Tannhäuser* to Paris in 1860, and to make it more popular with Parisians, who love ballet, he inserted a ballet in the first act. Unfortunately, Parisians also love to arrive fashionably late and see a ballet in the second act, so *Tannhäuser* was forced to close after just three performances.[40]

Beauty

• Marie Wilt was a 300-pound opera singer. In Vienna, where she was born in 1833, she sang the role of Valentino in *The Huguenots*. As she walked on stage, the character of the Page said the words the script required him to say and announced that she was the most beautiful lady at court. Of course, the audience started laughing, but they quickly stopped laughing when she sang. And given the way she sang, chances are that by the end of the opera some audience members — judging from their enthusiastic applause — thought that she really was the most beautiful woman at court! Ms. Wilt's first teacher was most unusual: an echo. Up on a mountain, she used to sing, listen to her echo, and then correct herself. (Nature can be a wonderful teacher!)[41]

• When Canadian figure skater Toller Cranston served as a judge at a Miss USA beauty pageant, the contestant from New York told him that she loved opera. However, in conversation, he found out that she had never been to the Met and that her favorite opera was *Phantom of the Opera*, so he told her, "My dear, don't even think about going to *La Traviata*. You would hate it."[42]

Children

• José Carreras discovered opera when he was a child. He saw the movie *The Great Caruso*, which starred Mario Lanza in the title role, and he started to sing the arias that he had heard in the movie. As a result, his family bought a record player and the soundtrack from the movie. Of course, as a child José did not sing as well as he did years later as a star of opera. He sometimes had to sing his favorite aria, "*La Donna è Mobile*," in the bathroom; however, he sometimes performed in his mother's salon, and her customers gave him small tips that he used to buy small toys and candy. As an adult, Mr. Carreras made his debut at La Scala as Riccardo in *Un Ballo in Maschera*. The great tenor Giuseppe di Stefano saw him in rehearsal and noticed that his costume did not fit well. Mr. di Stefano took him to his own vast costume collection and gave him a costume that fit him better — it was the same costume that Mr. di Stefano had worn in the same role when he performed at La Scala.[43]

• Conductor Walter Damrosch used to give the Siegfried whistle when he wanted his children to come to him. This whistle is the music that Siegfried blows on his horn when he calls the dragon to come and fight him. When his daughter Gretchen heard this music the first time she attended a performance of Wagner's *Siegfried*, she almost automatically got up to go to her father, and then she wondered how Siegfried had gotten ahold of her father's music. The Siegfried whistle came in handy at railway stations — it prevented the children from getting lost. While the family was traveling by train in Milan, Italy, Mr. Damrosch sounded the Siegfried whistle at a railway station, and an Italian who knew the music well answered him. One of the Damrosch daughters went to their father; the other three Damrosch daughters went to the musical Italian.[44]

• Leo Slezak and his wife sometimes allowed their children to bring cots into their room and sleep there. This worked well for their son, Walter, who slept soundly, but their daughter, Greterl, used to stay awake and wait for them to return home after a party. Mr. Slezak wanted her to get her rest, so he said that unless she went to sleep, she wouldn't be allowed to sleep in his and his wife's bedroom. The only result was that his daughter pretended to be asleep when he and his wife returned home. He used to ask, "Are you asleep, Greterl?" She would reply, "Yes, Daddy." Later, she wouldn't fall for that trick, so

Mr. Slezak would hold a chocolate under her nose and ask, "Have a chocolate?" Unable to resist the temptation, Greterl would open her eyes and pop the chocolate in her mouth.[45]

• Tenor Carlo Bergonzi knew early that he wanted to sing professionally. When he was 14 years old, he was working in a cheese factory, pushing a wheelbarrow and singing. However, his foreman stopped him and said, "One cannot do [two] things at once. One can either work, or sing." Immediately, young Carlo made up his mind: "In that case, I'd much rather sing!" Before going home, he told the story of his quitting to his father, who worked in the same cheese factory. His father approved of his decision: "Good. Now go home." The next day, Carlo auditioned for a singing teacher.[46]

• Even at a very early age, soprano Geraldine Farrar was determined to appear before the public. In 1892, when she was 10 years old, her hometown of Melrose, Massachusetts, decided to put on a celebration with schoolchildren representing the first 13 states. Her school had the honor of selecting a girl to participate. Geraldine was selected, and she represented Massachusetts on a float. Watching the float with black eyes — courtesy of Geraldine — were two little girls in her class who had not wanted her to be the girl participating in the celebration.[47]

• As a small boy, Andrea Bocelli spent time in a hospital because of his congenital bilateral glaucoma. His eyes hurt, and he was restless. However, his mother discovered that at times when he lay pressed against a wall he became relaxed, and when he moved away from the wall he cried. His mother moved next to the wall and concentrated. From the room next door came the faint sound of music. She went next door and requested permission to sometimes bring her son in to visit and to listen to the record player. In this way, young Andrea discovered music.[48]

• When Christine Nilsson was a child, her family was impoverished. One way they made money was to teach Christine and her brother a few songs, and whenever their mother saw a stranger coming, she had the children play music for him until he had given them money. Some strangers gave them money because the strangers liked their playing; others gave them money so that they would stop their playing. Later, she made great sums of money as an operatic soprano.[49]

• In the 1960s, while Schuyler Chapin was head of the Columbia Records Masterworks department, his family had an outing with the family of soprano Eileen Farrell. One of Mr. Chapin's sons, Sam, was just starting to learn how to tell jokes, and he asked Ms. Farrell, "Where does a 600-pound canary sit?" After hearing the answer, "Anywhere it wants to," Ms. Farrell asked him what a 600-pound canary would sound like. Sam didn't know, so Ms. Farrell said, "Like this," and she sang a high C that had Sam covering his ears.[50]

• On October 11, 1968, Plácido Domingo became the father of a boy, whom he named Alvaro. The very next night, Mr. Domingo sang at the New York City Opera in *Pagliacci*. He played the part of a clown, and in one scene he was supposed to throw candy to a chorus of children on stage, but on this night he instead threw cigars to the adults, including adults in the audience. Each cigar was marked, "It's a boy!"[51]

• When Maria Callas was a young girl, she and Jackie, her sister, were supposed to make their bed, but sometimes they forgot. Whenever that happened, their mother would go to their closet, take out their clothes, and put the clothes in the hallway. Maria and Jackie would come home, see the clothes, and say "Oh, Mother!" Then they would pick up their clothes, put them away, and make up their bed.[52]

• As a child, Gladys Ripley wanted to be a soprano, in part because she loved the "*Miserere*" duet from *Il Trovatore*, but nature insisted that she be a contralto. She was finally won over after hearing the singing of contralto Clara Butt. Ms. Ripley was impressed by the diamond tiara that Ms. Butt wore at the concert, she realized that contraltos could be important people, and she became a contralto.[53]

• Mariah Carey's mother, Patricia, sang with the New York City Opera, and of course she listened to recordings of opera at home, and sometimes she sang along. One day, she sang part of an aria, then she stopped, and Mariah sang the next line — in Italian! At the time, Mariah was not yet three years old![54]

• Antoine de Choudens was a music publisher who got rich from the French rights to Charles Gounod's *Faust*. However, Mr. Choudens did not like music. Whenever his children misbehaved, he used to threaten to take them to the opera unless they straightened up.[55]

Chapter 2: From Christmas to Divas

Christmas

• Conductor Walter Damrosch had four daughters, none of whom liked a Dr. Colton who was also a ladies' man. At a family dinner, the four daughters criticized Dr. Colton, pointing out his many weaknesses. The daughters' mother, Margaret Damrosch, told them, "Everyone around the table must say something nice about Dr. Colton." After a long silence, daughter Anita said, "Dr. Colton had a bath last Tuesday." Her mother said, "I forbid you to say that!" Anita then said, "Dr. Colton did not have a bath last Tuesday." Mr. Damrosch laughed. By the way, he used two of his daughters in small roles in the opera *The Children of Bethlehem*: Gretchen and young Polly. They and other children brought gifts for the infant Jesus. The other children were eight professional actors, including Tina, whose father was a very successful grocer. Gretchen wrote about the children who were professionals and had been taught by adult professionals that "when they acted, they were children imitating middle-aged men and women acting like children." During the performance, Gretchen gave the infant Jesus a doll that the soprano playing the Virgin Mary indicated should be placed on the lowest of some steps — this was not a position of honor. Tina's father the grocer really came through for her — she brought a cornucopia of colorful fruits and vegetables all piled high on a straw tray. The soprano playing the Virgin Mary indicated that this tray should be placed on the highest step — the position of honor. Gretchen wrote, "The Virgin had become a little excited over the offerings. She had apparently forgotten the waxen Baby by her side and was accepting the gifts as some sort of personal tribute." Polly, Gretchen's sister, had brought as a gift a cauliflower that her mother had bought for eighteen cents. The soprano playing the Virgin Mary did not motion for Polly to come forward, but young Polly walked up the steps and put the cauliflower in the cradle with Baby Jesus. Gretchen wrote, "Somehow she knew that He was nearer her own age and would understand. What she did not know was that she had unconsciously righted a scene and made it Christmas again."[56]

• Pianist Derek Smith reads music well and can play many different kinds of music, but he was worried when he was booked on almost no notice to accompany opera singer Luciano Pavarotti on the TV show *Good Morning America*. Opera music can be difficult to play, and Mr. Smith had no idea how difficult the music that Mr. Pavarotti would sing to would be, and no one at the TV studio seemed to know what Mr. Pavarotti was going to sing. Mr. Pavarotti showed up, but he quickly became surrounded by many people, so Mr. Smith could not get near him. Finally, Mr. Smith was able to get close enough to Mr. Pavarotti to ask, "Could I have a look at the sheet music?" He was handed a copy of the sheet music for "We Wish You a Merry Christmas."[57]

Clothing

• Ruggero Leoncavallo, composer of *Pagliacci*, once was asked by Emperor Wilhelm II of Germany to compose an opera. He composed *Der Roland von Berlin*, and he went to the German court to deliver the score. Because the Kaiser was busy, Mr. Leoncavallo was asked to wait with a number of other people, all of whom were wearing full-dress military uniforms, while he was wearing his usual somber black clothing. Of course, he stood out, and many chamberlains who saw him and thought that he did not belong in the company of those officers asked if he was supposed to be there. Mr. Leoncavallo said, "I found in the end that it saved time to keep my invitation card constantly in my hand, as no sooner had I put it back in than I had to take it out again to satisfy some other bespangled official that the right place for me was not the servants' hall." Of course, this was annoying, but soon Mr. Leoncavallo got satisfaction. The Kaiser arrived, complimented his score, and invited him to lunch. Mr. Leoncavallo says about the officials, "As soon as the Kaiser had gone, they all crowded around me smiling, smirking, scraping, bowing, as if I had suddenly become a second God the Father Almighty."[58]

• When the Metropolitan Opera moved to Lincoln Center, Leontyne Price starred in a Franco Zeffirelli production of *Antony and Cleopatra* that was plagued by mishaps. This cooled her relationship with the Met, and she devoted her gifts to the San Francisco Opera and other venues. However, when Schuyler Chapin became the Met's general manager, he wanted Ms. Price to sing at the Met, so he set up a luncheon with her at La Cote Basque, a fancy New York restaurant. Ms. Price wore elegant black pants and a mink coat, but when the manager of the La Cote Basque, Madame Henriette, saw her, she told Mr. Chapin to tell Ms. Price that women in pants could not eat there. Mr. Chapin pleaded, "Madame, if you deny Leontyne Price, I'll never be able to persuade her to return to the Metropolitan Opera. She asked to lunch at your restaurant. Please! We need her back on the Met stage. New York misses her. Help me!" Madame Henriette relented, saying, "Never let it be said that La Cote Basque has denied our city a great artist. I say rules can be bent!"[59]

• While singing for the troops in her native Australia during World War II (despite having contracted polio), opera soprano Marjorie Lawrence always wore lovely gowns. Keeping them pressed was not as much of a problem as it would seem because there was always a soldier or nurse who was willing to iron them. Once, a nurse took a gown to press it, but with the beginning of the concert approaching, the gown had not been returned, so Ms. Lawrence sent her husband after it. He found the nurse wearing it — and a half-dozen other nurses waiting for a chance to try it on. The nurse explained, "We've been out here in the wilderness nearly two years, and this is the first lovely dress we've seen since leaving home. I simply had to put it on."[60]

• During World War II, British civilians were trained to be members of the Home Guard. Soprano Joan Hammond was out for a walk one evening when a well-dressed man wearing a bowler hat and carrying an umbrella pointed his umbrella at her and said, "Boom! Boom! Boom!" Ms. Hammond thought that he was harmless, so she said, "I'm dead." The well-dressed man raised his bowler hat and said politely, "I beg your pardon, Madam, but there is a Home Guard exercise here this evening, and I thought you were one of the enemy." Ms. Hammond writes, "I was delighted with this bit of whimsy as there was an air raid in progress at the time, and here we were preparing for the invasion of Eaton Square, bowler hats and all."[61]

Competition

• In 1934, at the Opera of Chicago, tenor Joseph Benton, aka Giuseppe Bentonelli, sang the part of Mario Cavaradossi to the leading Tosca of his time. (Unfortunately, Mr. Benton doesn't reveal the name of the soprano playing Tosca.) During the first act, Mr. Benton was surprised by how tightly the Tosca was squeezing his rib cage. With a shock, he realized that she was trying to cut short his breath so that he couldn't hit an important high note. Having been raised a strong Oklahoma farm boy, he drew a deep breath despite her best efforts to prevent him, and he blasted the high note four inches from her right ear. She winced, but the audience applauded.[62]

• Lauritz Melchior and Maria Jeritza sang together in Richard Wagner's *Die Walküre*. In the opera, Ms. Jeritza finished singing, and then she lay at Mr. Melchior's feet as he sang a solo. However, Ms. Jeritza didn't like all the audience's attention being directed at Mr. Melchior, so she moved her skirt and revealed a long expanse of leg. Mr. Melchior saw what she was doing, so as he sang, he moved her skirt back over her legs. Again, Ms. Jeritza showed her legs, and again Mr. Melchior covered her legs. For the rest of the scene, the audience was treated to the sight of the two opera singers competing for their attention.[63]

• Early in his career, Farinelli sang an aria with a trumpet obbligato. Each night, there was a contest between Farinelli and the trumpet player. They would each take a deep breath, then Farinelli would sing a note accompanied by the trumpet player. Each night, the audience waited to see who would run out of breath first and lose the contest: Farinelli or the trumpet player. Each night, Farinelli won the contest.[64]

• Singers of opera can hate other singers. Mario Lanza, who sang opera in movies such as *The Great Caruso*, used to break the records of singers he didn't like in music stores. (If he was caught, he paid for the records he had broken.)[65]

Conductors

• Opera singer Nellie Melba noticed a youth who stared at her and followed her around during a time she was singing *Faust* at Covent Garden. She finally asked him who he was, and he replied that his name was Landon Ronald and he had just been engaged as *répétiteur* at Covent Garden. (*Répétiteurs* play piano at rehearsals and coach singers.) She asked, "Are you any good? [...] Do you know *Manon*?" (This opera was also being performed at Covent Garden.) He replied, "Yes," and she said to him, "Very well. Come to my hotel tomorrow at twelve o'clock, and I'll see what you are made of." He showed up, and he played the opening bars of *Manon* without any music in front of him. Ms. Melba said, "Not so fast. You have studied this. I haven't. I want the book." They went through the first act, and Ms. Melba said to Mr. Ronald, "You play beautifully, and you seem to have a wonderful memory. Have you studied *Manon* for long?" He replied, "No. I borrowed the score after the performance, and sat up learning it all last night. I had never seen it before." Of course, the young Mr. Ronald became a world-renowned conductor and composer. Ms. Melba said about this example of Mr. Ronald's work ethic, "And that is why Landon Ronald is Landon Ronald!" Of course, he did make mistakes when he was young. Everyone does. He once got in trouble while Giuseppe Campari was singing before a large audience. Mr. Ronald was unable to bring the orchestra and the singer together. Fortunately, Mr. Campari good-naturedly said, "I think we'll begin again." This time, all went well. And once Mr. Ronald played the accompaniment for Ms. Melba in the wrong key and she said to him, "Landon, please try the other key. I'm not a contralto yet!" (He had played the music for a contralto the previous night, and absent-mindedly played in the same key for Ms. Melba.) Ms. Melba believed that in cases of a mistake it is better to acknowledge it than to try to keep it secret from the audience. She said about Mr. Ronald's wrong key and its correction, "I need hardly say that every audience adores a little scene like that!"[66]

• Anton Seidl could be cutting in his wit. He once listened to a young woman sing, but the young woman lacked vocal talent. When she asked him for his advice, he replied, "I advise you to marry some rich old tradesman." She did. And when he wanted to conduct Richard Strauss' tone poem *Thus Spake Zarathustra*, but the price for doing so was exorbitant, he said, "I know that Zarathustra spoke a great deal. But he didn't say that much." Mr. Seidl loved Wagnerian opera. When he was with the Neumann Company, he was scheduled to conduct *Die Walküre* in Italy. The King of Italy promised to attend, and the Italian custom was to stop the performance of the opera when the King, who apparently was always fashionably late, walked in. The orchestra would play the *Marcia Reale* (the Royal March) and then resume the opera. Mr. Seidl absolutely declined to do this, and for the performance that the King attended, the assistant conductor took over and observed the Italian custom. By the way, the German operatic tenor Max Alvary greatly respected Mr. Seidl's conducting. A lesser conductor once criticized Mr. Alvary because he had not started singing when the conductor had indicated that he should come in with his first beat. Mr. Alvary replied, "The first beat! I am an actor! I have no time to watch your beats! I was waiting for the big wall of sound to plunge into it with my voice — but the wave never came." Mr. Alvary told music critic Henry T. Finck, "When Mr. Seidl conducts, these waves of sound, be they large or small, never fail to rise."[67]

• Richard Strauss had a rocky relationship with his wife, Pauline, and often he experienced senseless scenes with his wife yelling at him. Once, the Strausses and Lotte Lehmann were having coffee in a garden when rain suddenly arose, upsetting Pauline so much that she began yelling at her husband. Ms. Lehmann tried to defend him, saying, "But, Pauline, how can your husband stop the rain?" However, Mr. Strauss was used to bearing his wife's outbursts patiently and told Ms. Lehmann, "Don't defend me — that always makes it much worse." While conducting *Die Walküre* in Vienna, Mr. Strauss kept making faces. Ms. Lehmann thought that he was making faces at her because he didn't like the way she was singing, so she confronted him with an outburst after the opera. However, Mr. Strauss told her that he was making faces at a musician, and then he added that her outburst had amused him because it showed that not just his wife was capable of such senseless scenes.[68]

• In 1943 in Zurich, Switzerland, Sir Georg Solti first heard Hans Hotter, who was singing in a performance of *Die Walküre*. Sir Georg was impressed: "The intensity of his characterization, stage presence, musicality and the sheer vocal power was simply wonderful." Four years later in Munich, Germany, Sir Georg conducted his first *Die Walküre* — Mr. Hotter sang the part of Wotan. Later, they recorded the *Ring* for Decca. Sir Georg asked Mr. Hotter to sing in a particular way a passage in *Walküre*. Mr. Hotter said, "I don't think I have ever tried that before." Sir Georg replied, "I learned it from you!" By the way, throughout his career Mr. Hotter stayed in character as Wotan, king of the gods, even when appearing before the curtain and accepting the audience's applause. A critic once wrote about him at such a time, "Hotter looks as though the audience was a nasty smell."[69]

• Arturo Toscanini grew up in Parma, Italy, where the workers sang arias from the famous operas they loved. Unfortunately, mistakes occasionally crept into an aria due to the faulty memory of a worker. When young Toscanini heard his first opera, Giuseppe Verdi's *Un Ballo in Maschera*, he thought that the opera singers were singing it incorrectly because the workers he had listened to had sung an aria differently. Young Toscanini stood up and yelled, "No, no. You are wrong!" Then he sang the aria the way he thought it was supposed to be sung.[70]

• As is well known, Arturo Toscanini conducted from memory because of his poor eyesight. A musician once told conductor Karl Böhm that he had told Maestro Toscanini, "Of course, you know exactly how it goes, but you don't know each individual part by heart." Maestro Toscanini replied, "Give me a test." The musician said, "Write out for me, with the bar rests, the bassoon part from the fight scene in the second act of *Die Meistersinger*." This was a remarkable test — but Maestro Toscanini passed it.[71]

• Sir Thomas Beecham, the famous conductor, once was having a hard time getting along with soprano Grace Moore during a rehearsal of *Louise* at the New York Metropolitan Opera. During a break in rehearsal, Sir Thomas began to speak of other performances that he had conducted. At one, the tenor complained that the soprano was dying too soon. Sir Thomas' reply to the tenor was, "My dear Sir, no soprano ever dies too soon." This story caused Ms. Moore to laugh, and the two got along after that.[72]

• Arturo Toscanini was known for his fabulous memory, and he often memorized scores. At a performance of *Tosca*, he was seen consulting a score. During intermission, a couple of surprised music lovers asked one of the musicians if Toscanini was losing his memory. The musician replied, "No, the maestro is just running through *Tannhauser* for tomorrow night."[73]

• The great conductor Arturo Toscanini knew more than music. Once, he became greatly upset by a set design for a scene in *Faust*. He cried out, "Shame! Shame! This is no Elizabethan house. You know nothing! Read Shakespeare! Study Verdi! Then you will know what to do." He then declined to hold any rehearsals until a new, better set had been built.[74]

Costumes

• Opera singer Geraldine Farrar ran into problems with society women requesting the loan of her costumes to be used in programs to benefit charity. Early in her career, she granted these requests, but after several expensive costumes were returned in poor condition, she declined all of these requests. When a buxom woman wanted to borrow her second act *Tosca* costume and became obnoxious when she declined, Ms. Farrar told the woman, "Dear lady, until you can lift your façade and restrain your posterior, you would need not one but several of my *Tosca* dresses."[75]

• When soprano Beverly Sells was set to debut at La Scala, she had a problem with a wardrobe mistress. Ms. Sells had asked for a silver costume, but the costumer brought her a gold lamé costume at each rehearsal. At each rehearsal, the wardrobe mistress promised to have the silver costume ready at the next rehearsal, but she always brought the gold costume instead. Ms. Sells solved the problem by taking scissors and cutting the gold costume in half. The other opera singers cheered her, and she made her debut in a silver costume.[76]

• Giacomo Puccini's first big success was the opera *Manon Lescaut*, for which soprano Lucrezia Bori bought a beautiful dress in which to make her debut as Manon in a revival. Mr. Puccini visited her backstage, looked at the dress, and told her that it was too lovely — after all, her character was supposed to be penniless and starving. Then, to make the dress more suitable to her character, he splashed it with coffee. Ms. Bori was not pleased with Mr. Puccini's attention to detail.[77]

• When she was seven years old, Beverly Sills was fortunate enough to see and hear Lily Pons in *Lakmé* at the New York Metropolitan Opera House. At her entrance, Ms. Pons made a major impression on the audience because her costume included a brief halter top, lots of skin, and a silken wrap around her hips. Young Beverly exclaimed, "Mama! Mama! Her belly button is showing!"[78]

• African-American opera singer Grace Bumbry knew how to get publicity. In London, she promised the press that when she danced the Dance of the Seven Veils, she would end up wearing nothing but "jewels and perfume." In fact, she ended up wearing a bikini covered with jewels — to the delight of the audience. Afterward, Ms. Bumbry laughed as she said, "They never sold so many binoculars."[79]

Critics

• Criticism can be funny, it can be devastating, and it can be educational. (So can insults.) Sometimes the accompanist is much better than the singer: Henry Bird once told a singer, "Young lady, I have tried playing for you on the white notes, I have tried playing for you on the black notes, but I simply cannot play in the cracks." At first, cellist Emanuel Feuermann received bad reviews of his concerts in London — he even thought of no longer playing in London. After reading one review of his playing, he told accompanist Gerald Moore, "If a pupil of mine received that notice, I would tell him to give up the cello." While Feodor Chaliapin was rehearsing Nikolai Rimsky-Korsakov's opera *Mozart et Salieri*, he wanted the orchestra to play at the tempo he wanted, so he gestured at the orchestra and stamped his feet in the tempo he wanted. The conductor said to him, "Kindly remember that I am the conductor," and Mr. Chaliapin replied, "In a garden where there are no birds, a croaking toad is a nightingale." The insulted conductor left the building, and the rehearsal ended. Gerald Moore accompanied Mr. Chaliapin during concerts, and they respected each other. Mr. Chaliapin was never impatient with Mr. Moore, but he did criticize him when he felt that criticism was needed. During one rehearsal, he said to Mr. Moore after he played the long pianoforte introduction to the classical French love song *"Plasir d'amour"* by Jean-Paul-Égide Martini, "Not just the notes. Not just the notes." In *Am I Too Loud?*, one of his autobiographies,

Mr. Moore wrote, "It can be so beautiful if played thoughtfully and expressively but my uninformed strumming made it sound commonplace. I took it home to think about it and ever since that episode I have devoted more time, more practice, more concentration to the music that looks easy. The average accompanist, I am afraid, only practises with diligence that which *looks* difficult." Of course, some critics can be partial. After a concert by contralto Astra Desmond, her 10-year-old son told a bunch of taxi drivers outside the concert hall, "My mother is the greatest singer in all space."[80]

• After a performance, Leontyne Price greatly enjoyed hearing praise from members of the audience and she greatly disliked hearing criticism from members of the audience. After one performance, she was speaking to a line of members of the audience and one man near the end of the line started waving at her. Ms. Price thought that here was one man who had greatly enjoyed the performance and was going to tell her how great she was, but when the man finally spoke to her, he asked, "Miss Price, did I detect a slight strain on your B-flat in the aria?" Ms. Price smiled at him and said, "Would you do me a small favor and get quietly out of the line so the other people can tell me beautiful things about my B-flat?" (Actually, she admits that she was "rougher than that" on the man. She told an interviewer, "I'll never tell what I said to him. It was bad — straight to the jugular vein.")[81]

• Eileen Farrell was a favorite opera soprano of flutist Donald Peck, and he once performed with her. Afterward, he went backstage and complimented her on her singing. She was very nice and said that she was surprised by his big flute tone because his body was so slim. He replied, "But Miss Farrell, you have such a huge voice!" She joked, "Yes, but I am as wide as you are tall!" By the way, a young cellist with the Chicago Symphony Orchestra did not realize that opera singers will often not sing in full voice during rehearsal, and so he was unimpressed with Ms. Farrell during rehearsal and remarked, "So, what's so great about Eileen Farrell?" But during the actual performance, she did sing with her full voice, and the cellist was properly impressed and remarked, "I can't hear myself. Am I playing?" This was a charming way of admitting that he had been mistaken earlier.[82]

• Violinist Jascha Heifetz and tenor John McCormack once sailed together on a ship to Monte Carlo. They got together in a cabin and had a fun time singing and playing music. Suddenly, they realized that it was dawn! Unfortunately, not everyone had had the fun time that they had had. Their neighbor complained to the room steward, "What the devil was going on all night? One gent caterwauling and another gent scraping a fiddle. I never got a wink of sleep." The room steward told him, "That was Jascha Heifetz and John McCormack." The irate man replied, "When I get home, I'm going to smash every d*mn record I own of either of them!"[83]

• Musician and impresario Maurice Strakosch once took opera singer Adelina Patti, before she was famous, to sing to Gioachino Rossini. She sang for him a song from Rossini's *Barber of Seville*: "*Una vove poco fa.*" However, Mr. Strakosch had embellished the song greatly with fancy "improvements." Mr. Rossini kept praising the singing: "*Brava*! *Bravissia*!" After Ms. Patti had finished singing, Mr. Rossini said to her, "Beautiful voice! Excellent method!" Then Mr. Rossini, a master of sarcasm, added, "And what a brilliant and effective song! Pray tell me the name of the composer."[84]

• Opera singers sometimes have jokes that they play on stage. While singing opposite Siegfried Jerusalem in a performance of *Tristan* at Bayreuth, soprano Waltraud Meier shocked conductor Daniel Barenboim by substituting a line from an operetta for a line from *Tristan*. She says, "I've always wanted to sing that — once! It rhymes better!" In addition, Ms. Meier says, Siegfried Jerusalem, who was singing the role of Tristan, sang about spaghetti in the second act. By the way, he says that no critic noticed.[85]

• Richard Barthelemy, the voice coach and accompanist of Enrico Caruso, was aware that many opera patrons had little to no knowledge of opera. He was invited to lunch with one such high-society opera patron the day after a new Italian opera premiered. He asked her for her opinion of the opera, but she replied, "It's impossible to give you an opinion — I haven't yet read the reviews in the morning papers."[86]

• Rudolf Bockelmann, a German dramatic baritone best known for his roles in Richard Wagner's operas, did not read English, but he closely examined his critical notices in London newspapers. Classical record producer Walter Legge wrote that Mr. Bockelmann would search for the word *but*: "If he found it, he grunted in German, 'It's all sh*t anyway.'"[87]

• Early in her career, soprano Rita Hunter read a review that stated, "If Miss Hunter persists in singing her top notes with such abandon, she won't have a voice at all in two years." Thirty years later, she still had her voice. She also still had the review — which she displayed on a wall in her bathroom.[88]

• When press releases announced that the petite Lily Pons would make her debut in the title role of *Carmen*, the critic of the Boston *Transcript*, H.T. Parker, said, "Thank God! At last we'll have a Carmen who weighs less than the bull!"[89]

Death

• Domenico Gaetano Maria Donizetti (1797-1848) wrote 75 operas and influenced Giuseppe Verdi. When he died, he was given an autopsy during which the top of his skull was removed. When his body was dug up in 1875 so that it could be moved to another location, the top of his skull was discovered to be missing. It turned out that an Austrian military physician named Gerolamo Carchen, who had watched the autopsy, had taken the piece of skull as a souvenir. For several years, the piece of skull was exhibited in a Bergamo museum dedicated to Donizetti, and then in 1951 it was buried with the rest of his bones.[90]

• On November 29, 1924, Giacomo Puccini died. However, he left behind him one last musical masterpiece. On April 25, 1926, in

Milan, Arturo Toscanini conducted the world premiere of *Turandot*. When the last note of the opera was finished, Maestro Toscanini told the audience, "Here the master laid down his pen."[91]

• This anecdote is touching. After Enrico Caruso died, his widow, Dorothy, played one of his recordings. Their young daughter, Gloria, heard the recording and toddled into the room, holding her arms up and saying, "Daddy! Daddy!"[92]

Divas

• Alexander Woollcott was seldom abashed by the great personalities of the arts, but when Grace Moore and he, along with other notables such as Harpo Marx, were invited to a luncheon with the great soprano Mary Garden, he was quiet at the luncheon — something very unusual for him. Ms. Garden, annoyed at Mr. Woollcott, did all the talking, telling the story of how she became famous by singing the role of Louise after the original soprano suffered from laryngitis. On that night, Albert Carré, the director of the Opéra Comique, came looking for her, telling her, "You have to go on as Louise. I've been told you've learned the role." As she prepared to go on, she told herself, "Mary Garden, this is your moment. Tomorrow Paris will be at your feet!" All happened as she had predicted. She scored a major success, and all the opera lovers of Paris adored her. After Ms. Garden had told this tale, Mr. Woollcott, thinking that it would make a wonderful magazine article, said, "My God, what a story — what a beginning!" Ms. Garden looked at him and said, "But that, my dear Woollcott, is a story which you cannot use in *Cosmopolitan* or any other magazine." As Mr. Woollcott and Ms. Moore drove away after the luncheon, he told her, "Well, regardless of my apparent lack of success, there is the most charming and eloquent b*tch I have ever met."[93]

• Once a diva, always a diva. When soprano Nellie Melba appeared for the last time at Covent Garden, she gave a remarkable performance, and she seemed overwhelmed at the applause she received at the end of *La Bohéme*. The stagehands were worried that she would collapse because of all her emotion, so they drew the curtains. Ms. Melba immediately recovered completely and snapped at the stagehands, "Pull back those bloody curtains at once!" They did so, and in front of the audience she once again seemed overwhelmed by emotion and about to collapse.[94]

• Maria Callas once appeared at the Chicago Lyric Theater in *Madama Butterfly*. Backstage, while she was still dressed in her kimono costume, a law official served her with a subpoena regarding a breach of contract. Aghast, she stormed at the law official, "How dare you! I am a goddess!" Of course, many members of the media were present, and of course, as anyone familiar with the work of theatrical guru Danny Newman would guess, it was Mr. Newman who had alerted the media to be present at the diva's display of fireworks.[95]

• Opera is known for its divas. For example, soprano Kathleen Battle of the Metropolitan Opera of New York once rode in a limousine in which the air conditioning was set too high. She telephoned her manager to request that she telephone the chauffeur and order that the air conditioning be turned down.[96]

• Italian diva Angelica Catalani once complained about a rug that had been placed on stage, saying that it was not good enough for her to place her feet on. After her complaints, the rug was taken away and thereafter she placed her feet on a rare Italian scarf.[97]

Chapter 3: From Education to Kisses

Education

• Russian bass Feodor Chaliapine studied under Professor Dimitri Usatov, who was sometimes very severe and even hit him with his baton. In self-defense, Mr. Chaliapine sometimes stood behind the piano, which was close to the wall. Because Professor Usatov was stout, he was unable to get close enough to Mr. Chaliapine to hit him. One day, however, Professor Usatov was so angry that he shouted, "Come out of that, you young devil! Come out! I know your game!" Mr. Chaliapine came out, Professor Usatov beat him with his baton, and then they continued the lesson. (Professor Usatov was actually very kind, giving Mr. Chaliapine voice lessons for free and even teaching him table manners.)[98]

• Schuyler Chapin held many important jobs in the arts, including cultural affairs commissioner of New York City, Dean of the School of the Arts at Columbia University, and General Manager of the Metropolitan Opera. He fell in love with music early. Unfortunately, he discovered that he had no talent in music composition. Nadia Boulanger at the Longy School of Music in Cambridge agreed. She looked over some compositions of his, and then told him bluntly, "It's very simple. You have no talent." She thought that he ought to be an impresario instead. Mr. Chapin agreed. He says, "If you know you don't have talent yourself, you try to acquire the talent of recognizing talent in others."[99]

• One of the people who helped develop Australian soprano Joan Sutherland's voice was Richard Bonynge, who became her husband. He felt that she could sing higher, so he took advantage of the fact that she lacked perfect pitch. Placing her in such a way that she could not see the keyboard of the piano as she did her vocal exercises, he would play E flat and tell her that it was C, which she would reproduce. They continued in this way higher and higher, and eventually Mr.

Bonynge would reveal to her how high she was singing. In this way she developed her ability to sing notes much higher than she had thought she was capable of singing.[100]

• Every opera singer will crack on a note in public. Early in his career, while singing in Tel Aviv, Israel, Plácido Domingo cracked on two notes while singing an important aria in Charles-François Gounod's *Faust*, for which he had had inadequate time to prepare. He was horribly embarrassed, and he offered to resign from the Hebrew National Opera, but the directors would not accept his resignation. Instead, they said to him, "Plácido, here you have a chance to learn, and one mistake means nothing. We trust you, and we want you to continue." This vote of confidence, Plácido says, is "the biggest boost anyone has ever given me."[101]

• Mario Lanza was not good at reading music, so he learned new arias by listening to recordings by accomplished opera singers. Leila Edwards listened to him sing some arias from the role of Pinkerton in *Madama Butterfly*, and then she told him, "You learned from the [Beniamino] Gigli recording." Mr. Lanza asked, "How did you know?" Ms. Edwards replied, "Because you're making the same mistakes Gigli made!" (Mr. Lanza made his only appearances on an operatic stage as Pinkerton in *Madama Butterfly* in New Orleans on April 8 and April 10, 1948.)[102]

• Lotte Lehmann was a glorious lieder singer. Once she gave a master class at the Academy of the West, and Anna Russell, a singer of parodies of opera, asked to sit in on the class. Ms. Lehmann taught the class, then near the end she asked Ms. Russell to come forward. Ms. Lehmann then took Ms. Russell through the comic song *"Schlumph ist mein Gesitzenbaum"* (German for "Dumb is my sittingtree") and taught her to sing it much better than she had ever sung it before.[103]

• As a young man, Mario del Monaco entered a competitive examination at the Opera School in Rome. He sang successfully and won a scholarship. Unfortunately, when lessons commenced, Mr. del

Monaco became convinced that his teacher was ruining his voice. Eventually, he became so angry that he threw the score of *La Favorita* at his teacher's head![104]

• The singer and composer Nicola Porpora took the castrato Gaetano Caffarelli as a pupil, and made him sing for six years a single lesson based on vowel sounds. At the end of the six years, Mr. Porpora told his pupil, "I have nothing further to teach you — you are the greatest singer in the world."[105]

Embarrassment

• Kirsten Flagstad once recorded a number of arias in three hours of hard work, then she and Charles O'Connell, the man in charge of the recording, went to lunch. He asked if she were tired, and she explained that she was not tired vocally, but that a certain muscle ached from standing. She then took his hand, put it on her inner thigh, and said, "The muscle is all stiffened up. Can't you feel that muscle?" Mr. O'Connell could feel the muscle, and he almost died of embarrassment as all the people in the Waldorf dining room stared at them.[106]

• Tenor Franco Corelli could be brutally honest as a voice teacher. During a class, a young woman sang for him for the first time. Unfortunately, she was not good. Mr. Corelli asked her, "You have a singing teacher?" The woman nodded that yes, she did. Mr. Corelli then asked, "And you pay such a teacher?" Embarrassed — as was Mr. Corelli — she started crying and ran back to her seat.[107]

Etiquette, Lack of

• Opera/lieder singer Kathleen Ferrier had an interesting way of handling rude people. Following one of her concerts, a man in the audience met her in the artists' room and told her, "Miss Ferrier, I wanted to come round to tell you that it is a pity you included Schubert's '*Erlkönig*' in your program this evening; it is a hateful song and I detest it." Ms. Ferrier simply looked at him and asked, "And?" Of course, the man had nothing to reply to this mild, but effective, rebuff.[108]

• Arturo Toscanini had a policy of allowing no encores, as he felt they interfered with the flow of the operas he conducted. Unfortunately, on the very last night of the 1902-1903 season, the La Scala audience insisted on the encore of a favorite aria from *A Masked Ball*. Toscanini tried several times to continue, but he was unable. Finally, he ran from the podium in disgust and an assistant conductor finished the opera.[109]

• Even as a young girl, opera singer Maria Callas was assertive. A friend of the family used to come to her home and put his feet up on a table pedestal — something no one else was allowed to do. Young Maria was angered by this and told him, "Please don't put your feet on our nice furniture." When her mother told her to be nice, young Maria replied, "If you won't talk to him, Mother, I will."[110]

Gifts

• Giuseppe Campanari acted and sang the part of Kothner the final time that Anton Seidl conducted *Die Meistersinger* at the Metropolitan. Kothner appears in the first act but does not afterward appear in the opera until very much later in the final act, where the character waves a flag and sings a few notes. Mr. Campanari asked Mr. Seidl for permission to go home after the first act, thinking that in the final act a member of the chorus could very well wave the flag and sing the few notes. Mr. Seidl, however, replied, "No. Remain for the master's sake! [The master, of course, is the composer of *Die Meistersinger*: Richard Wagner.] Go to your dressing room, and I will send you something to keep you company." Mr. Campanari did retire to his dressing room, and Mr. Seidl sent him two cigars and a bottle of champagne with his compliments. Mr. Campanari writes, "At the proper moment, during the last act, the original Kothner appeared and thus Wagner's dignity was upheld at the expense of Mr. Seidl's purse." By the way, Mr. Seidl celebrated Christmas with a huge Christmas tree, and presents for his dogs — each dog got a sausage — hung on its branches.[111]

• In 1969, when opera singer Beverly Sills made her debut at La Scala in Milan, Italy, she and her daughter, Muffy, stayed in a hotel on a street that was famous for its flashily dressed prostitutes, all of whom carried large handbags. Muffy was very impressed with the glamour of the prostitutes, and she asked her mother, "Mama, how do you say 'beautiful' in Italian?" Ms. Sills answered, *Bella, bella.*" The next evening Muffy went over to a prostitute and told her, "*Bella, bella.*" The prostitute was so pleased that she reached into her handbag and pulled out a gift for Muffy: a piece of chocolate.[112]

• Bass singer Feodor Chaliapin once spent the night with a young woman, and the next morning he said, "I shall give you tickets for the opera this evening." Hinting for a different kind of gift, the woman told him that the opera tickets would be of no use to her as she was poor and hungry. Mr. Chaliapin replied, "If you wanted bread, you should have spent the night with a baker."[113]

Good Deeds

• When he was a very young man who had just graduated from Harvard, future music critic Henry T. Finck decided to attend the first Beyreuth Festival, with Richard Wagner himself conducting. He arrived several weeks before the festival began, and he wanted to attend the rehearsals of the great works of opera written by Mr. Wagner. No one was supposed to be admitted to the rehearsals, but he found a convenient keyhole and put his ear up to it. Someone discovered him doing this and said, "Nobody is allowed in here." Henry pointed out that he had spent a great amount of money for tickets to all the public performances of the festival, but to no avail. The attendant said, "I am extremely sorry, sir, but I have strict orders to make no exceptions. Fortunately, Henry met Mr. Wagner himself. He took the opportunity to ask the great man to allow him to attend rehearsals. At first, Mr. Wagner declined, thinking that Henry was a critic. (Henry became a critic — as which he was a defender of Wagner — later.) Henry said, "But I am not a critic, only a young man of 22 who has come simply to describe the new works." (True. Henry could write, and he had arranged to send articles about the festival to the *New York World* and *Atlantic Monthly*.) This pleased Mr. Wagner, who asked him, "Have you a *Patronatsschein*?" Henry replied, "Three!" Mr. Wagner then did a good deed. He said, "I had made up my mind to admit no one to the rehearsals, not even Liszt. But he has gone in and I have admitted a few others, so you might as well come, too." Mr. Finck wrote in his autobiography that he "had the time of my life watching the great master superintending every detail of the performances."[114]

• Lucrezia Bori of the Metropolitan Opera had surgery to remove some nodules from her vocal chords; unfortunately, the operation was not a success and she lost her singing and her speaking voice. Internationally famous Australian opera star Nellie Melba visited her and told her about the time that she had strained her voice by trying to sing a Wagnerian role that was not suited for her voice. For three months, she had remained completely silent, and she had recovered her voice. She added, "You are not yet thirty. Have patience. Wait and watch and work mentally. You will have a great future one day." In fact, that is what happened. Ms. Bori had another operation, and after lots of rest and silence, she was able to recover her voice and have a second career singing at the Met. When Ms. Bori returned to the Met, Ms. Melba was there. Before Ms. Bori's performance, Ms. Melba sent her a large basket of flowers, and after the performance, she told her, "You sang beautifully tonight. You are more marvelous than ever."[115]

• When Ivan Jadan, the premier lyric tenor of the Bolshoi Opera from 1928-1941, escaped from the rule of the dictator Josef Stalin in November of 1941, he walked west with a group of other artists and their families. As they neared an overturned German truck, one of the children in the group started crying. Hearing the child, a German soldier inside the truck stuck his head out of a door. The one member of the Russian group who could speak German asked in what direction they should travel. Although the Russians were supposed to be the enemies of the Germans, the German soldier saved their lives by warning him about a minefield directly ahead of them. Hearing the child cry had made the German soldier realize that these Russians needed help, and he gave it to them.[116]

• During World War 1, opera tenor Enrico Caruso visited a hospital for wounded veterans. He learned that a soldier who had lost his legs in the war was traveling through New York on his way to Washington, DC, for artificial legs. He also learned that the soldier wanted to see New York City. No problem. Mr. Caruso simply requested, "Put him in my car." Mr. Caruso and the veteran had lunch together, and then Mr. Caruso went to a rehearsal and his chauffeur took the veteran around New York and showed him the sights. Afterward, Mr. Caruso received a letter from the veteran: "Many thanks for your great kindness to me. When I get my new legs from Washington, I am coming to hear you sing."[117]

• An impoverished German student once wrote Jenny Lind, the 19th-century singer known as the Swedish Nightingale, begging for a ticket and promising to pay her for it when he received his allowance. Ms. Lind not only sent him two free tickets, but during the concert she made sure to smile in the direction of those particular seats.[118]

Fathers

• Tenor Manuel Garcia could be a very harsh teacher of singers. Often, the sound of crying could be heard at his house. People who asked the neighbors what was happening were told, "Oh, that's nothing. It's only Mr. Garcia teaching his pupils how to sing." He could also be more than harsh when teaching his own children. He once ordered his contralto daughter, Maria Felicita Malibran, whose voice extended into the soprano range, to learn an entirely new role in a few days. She protested because of the shortness of time, so he threatened to kill her if she did not learn the role. She learned the role. Despite this harsh treatment, she loved her father. Near the end of his career, they sang together — he as Otello and she as Desdemona. After a curtain call, her face appeared as dark as her father's. While the curtain was down, she had kissed his sooty face.[119]

• Danny O'Mara, a baritone, once sang a role in *Fidelio* that required his character to be in prison. His family frequently saw him play the role, and on a crowded bus returning home after a performance, one of his children complained loudly, "Why is it, every time we see Daddy, he's always in prison?"[120]

Food

• During a visit to his native Naples, Enrico Caruso invited a number of friends and acquaintances to lunch at a restaurant. Of course, these friends and acquaintances wanted to hear him sing, and he willingly sang both operatic arias and Neapolitan songs. One particular part of his audience gratified him, as he explained to his friend Salvatore Cortesi: "The cook's praise is the praise I love and respect most of all. Women will even weep as I sing, but they largely do that because it is Caruso that sings. But if I can draw the man who cooks my macaroni from his fire and if I can make him forget that there is such a thing as food in the world, then I know that I am touching the heights of my art."[121]

• A man named Bertani once wrote Giuseppe Verdi a letter in which he complained that Verdi's opera *Aida* lacked quality, despite his having heard it twice. In the letter, he enclosed a statement of the costs of hearing the opera, including the price of his opera tickets, the cost of the railroad tickets, and the cost of his evening meals after hearing the opera. Finally, he asked Verdi to reimburse his expenses. Verdi agreed, but he first extracted the promise that the man would never attend one of his operas again. In addition, he refused to pay for the cost of the evening meals, saying, "He could have perfectly well eaten at home."[122]

• Salvatore Baccaloni, a comedian in basso roles, was a huge man, weighing in at 325 pounds. During the mid-1950s, he confessed that the saddest day of his life was when his doctor placed him on a diet that stressed consumption of fruits and vegetables. What was the happiest day of his life? When he went off the diet. On that day, he enjoyed himself by consuming four pizzas, a meal with three kinds of meat, and one-half pound of a dessert cheese — Italian, of course.[123]

• Sir Rudolf Bing took steps to integrate the Metropolitan Opera, hiring such African-American divas as Leontyne Price. Whenever the Met toured, he set the policy that the Met would not stay at segregated hotels or perform in front of segregated audiences. Once, before the Met left to perform in Atlanta, Georgia, Ms. Price remarked to him, "I am sure that you will find room for the horse and me." In Atlanta, Sir Rudolf took her to dinner in the hotel. He says, "As we walked in, there was a sudden hush, which I greatly enjoyed."[124]

• Robert Merrill once worked with soprano Eileen Farrell, who had large breasts. During a rehearsal of one scene of *Forza*, Mr. Merrill's character was dying and over him was Ms. Farrell, whose breasts kept dipping before his face. Finally, Mr. Merrill asked her if she had "a cookie to go with the milk." A good sport, Ms. Farrell brought him a cookie on opening night.[125]

• Frances Alda and Kirsten Flagstad once dined together at the Ritz-Carlton, and the waiter asked Ms. Alda if she wanted to order Melba toast. This was a mistake, for Ms. Alda and Nellie Melba, after whom Melba toast was named, had been great rivals as opera singers. Ms. Alda roared at the waiter, "Melba toast! No! Bring Alda toast!"[126]

• Operatic tenor Jan Kiepura strongly preferred European sweet butter to American salted butter. At a restaurant, Mr. Kiepura pointed to some American salted butter and asked a server, "What is that?" Of course, the server replied, "That is butter, sir." Mr. Kiepura then said venomously, "In Poland, we give such butter to *pigs*!"[127]

• Operatic tenor Leo Slezak was a big man — six-foot-four and almost 300 pounds. His friends used to joke that it was cheaper to take a vacation trip to Cairo than to treat him to a meal. Whenever several citizens from Brünn showed up in Cairo, Mr. Slezak's friends joked that he must be singing in Brünn.[128]

Friends

• This anecdote may not be true, but it is a good one. One day, tenors John McCormack and Enrico Caruso met on the street. Mr. McCormack asked, "How is the world's greatest tenor?" Mr. Caruso answered, "And since when have you become a baritone?" By the way, much earlier in Mr. McCormack's life, from the gallery at Covent Garden he watched the great Enrico Caruso, and he vowed to his wife, "If I ever get my foot down there, it'll take a h*ll of a lot to get it off."[129]

• Luciano Pavarotti was forced to share a bedroom in a crowded hotel one night with his friend Franco "Panocia" Casarini. Unfortunately, they quickly discovered that each of them snored — loudly. After trying unsuccessfully to sleep at the same time, they ended up taking turns sleeping. Mr. Pavarotti slept for an hour, then Mr. Casarini slept for an hour, and so on until morning.[130]

Humility

• Soprano Marcella Sembrich managed not to let herself be overly impressed by the fame of other people or of herself. As a young student, she had the opportunity to demonstrate her talents before Franz Liszt. She wrote a friend, "Professor Schell, who takes great interest in me, wants me to meet Liszt when he comes. He wants me to sing and play for him. They say I can reach great achievement — but enough of that — what news of your garden?" Even after becoming famous, she retained her humility. When W.J. Henderson praised her by saying she was the most moving Violetta he had ever seen in *La Traviata*, she replied simply, "Don't you remember [Adelina] Patti?" This humble personality may be one reason why, when Ms. Sembrich retired from opera in 1909 with a farewell performance at the Metropolitan Opera in one act each from *Don Pasquale*, *Il Barbiere di Siviglia*, and *La*

Traviata, Geraldine Farrar honored her by singing the small role of Flora in act 1 of *La Traviata*.[131]

• Opera/lieder singer Kathleen Ferrier was humble. At an airport where she was landing, she looked out of the window of the airplane and saw a fancy reception committee on the ground. She told her companion, "Look at all the kerfuffle. There must be someone of importance on board." She looked around at the people on the airplane, then pointed to a portly man and said, "Probably a statesman or some industrial nabob." After the airplane had landed, she learned that the reception committee was for her.[132]

Husbands and Wives, and Wives and Wives

• In 1997, Patricia Racette and Beth Clayton, both opera singers and both lesbians, performed together in Verdi's *La Traviata* in Santa Fe. They had not known each other before, but they did meet at a party before production started on the opera. Ms. Racette remembers, "It was pretty clear that there was a lot of energy there. And then we got together in the summer and we started our staging, and it was lots of fireworks. It was pretty palpable. It was just a matter of time — let's put it that way." It didn't take much time. In the opera, Ms. Racette played Violetta, and Ms. Clayton played Flora, Violetta's best friend. In the opera, Violetta falls in love with the main male character, Alfredo, but on the opera stage, Ms. Racette and Ms. Clayton fell in love. At one point, Violetta was unconscious and Flora picked her up — and Flora gave Violetta a kiss. Ms. Racette says, "I was on the floor with Beth and, per the staging, she comes in and scoops me up. But she leaned over and just plants one on me! I had to turn my entire body into her because I couldn't stop laughing when I was supposed to be passed out!" In 2005, the two women had a commitment ceremony. Ms. Clayton says, "We had a reception, and we had a beautiful dinner, and my parents paid for it; that was not our plan, but they sort of came through in that Southern tradition. It was very affirming and validating."[133]

• Soprano Rosa Ponselle sang for herself after retiring from singing for opera audiences. When Rosa was approaching her 80th birthday, *Washington Post* music critic Paul Hume dropped by her house and heard lovely singing and thought, *Rosa's found a wonderful pupil.* Actually, Rosa herself was singing. Of course, she was wonderful on the stage and could wonderfully express emotion with her voice. At one time, getting a divorce was very difficult, but a divorce would be granted if either the husband or the wife had committed adultery. After English music critic Ernest Newman heard Rosa sing her first *Amore dei Tre Re* (*The Love of Three Kings*), an opera by Italo Montemezzi, he said, "If as a divorce-court judge, I had heard her one 'Ritorniam' breathed to her lover, I would have given her husband a divorce without hearing further evidence."[134]

• Composer and conductor Richard Strauss once had a terrible and very public quarrel with soprano Pauline de Ahna during a rehearsal. Because Fräulein de Ahna felt that Strauss was conducting the music too fast, she shouted insults at him from the stage, then went to her dressing room. Strauss followed her and for a long time shouting was heard from the dressing room, then silence fell. Members of the orchestra were upset at Fräulein de Ahna's conduct, and so a delegation knocked on her dressing room door, which was opened by Strauss. The delegation explained that in light of what had just happened, they felt that they could no longer work with Fräulein de Ahna. Strauss replied, "That hurts me very much because I have just become engaged to Fräulein de Ahna."[135]

• Tenor Franco Corelli suffered from stage fright before performances and even before making a recording. He was once scheduled to record an album of duets with Renata Tebaldi for Decca. Everything was ready for the recording, and everyone was ready except for Mr. Corelli, who was downstairs. Suddenly, the people in the recording studio heard a slap-slap, then they heard Mr. Corelli's wife tell her husband, "Now go upstairs and do it." As usual, Mr. Corelli was suffering from stage fright, and his wife had slapped him to get him to sing. Of course, when he did sing, he sang beautifully.[136]

• When opera singer Plácido Domingo was courting Marta Ornelas, he followed the Spanish custom of the serenade. He hired a mariachi band, positioned it under Ms. Ornelas' window, and then sang to her. She found this charming, but her neighbors did not, and they called the police. However, when the police found out that the serenader was Mr. Domingo, they asked the neighbors why they were complaining. After all, they were hearing a free concert by a gifted opera star of the Mexican National Opera. By the way, the serenade was successful. In 1962, Mr. Domingo and Ms. Ornelas were married.[137]

• Tenor Hugues Cuenod sang the part of Styx in Jacques Offenbach's *Orpheus in the Underworld* with Teresa Stich-Randall at the Grand Theater in Geneva. During celebrations for New Year's, Mr. Cuenod decided to make a play on the names "Stich" and "Styx," so he sang, "Listen, if you marry me, you will have almost nothing to change on your calling card!" Both Ms. Stich and the audience enjoyed the joke.[138]

• Enrico Caruso once took his wife, Dorothy, out to buy furs. They went to an expensive store, and several furs were laid out before her. He asked her, "Which you like?" She named the shortest fur, because she thought that it would be the least expensive. Mr. Caruso then turned to the store attendant and said, "We will take them all."[139]

Illnesses and Injuries

• In the summer of 1987, opera tenor José Carreras discovered that he had leukemia. He underwent chemotherapy in Barcelona, Spain, where he sang arias as a way of timing how much longer the chemo sessions would last. The chemo was not completely effective, so he went to Seattle, Washington, where he had a bone marrow transplant. Lots of fans wrote him while he was in the hospital — he even received a letter addressed simply to "Tenor, Seattle." His rival tenors, Plácido Domingo and Luciano Pavarotti, came through for him. Mr. Pavarotti sent him this telegram: "José, get well. Otherwise, I won't have any competition." Mr. Domingo frequently telephoned him and also flew to Seattle to visit him.[140]

• Opera singer Pasquale Brignoli was traveling on a train in Pennsylvania when he decided to smoke a cigarette while standing on the outside platform of the rear car. Unfortunately, while he was lighting his cigarette, the train jolted and Brignoli tumbled over onto the railroad tracks. Cries immediately rang out: "Stop the train! Brignoli's been killed!" Suddenly, everyone heard Brignoli singing loud, full, and clear. He then prayed, "I thank thee, Lord! My body has suffered grievously; but the voice — ah, the voice! — has not been injured."[141]

Insults

• French opera singer Sophie Arnould's insults could be stunning. Mlle. Guimard used to dance at the Paris Opera in the 18th century. Her dancing consisted mostly of graceful arm movements — she used her feet very little when she danced. When Ms. Arnould heard that during a rehearsal a piece of scenery had fallen and broken Mlle. Guimard's arm, she commented, "It's a pity that it wasn't her leg; then it wouldn't have interfered with her dancing." And when a friend mentioned a diamond necklace that an actress had been given by her lover, saying that the necklace was so long that it almost reached the actress' waist, Ms. Arnould commented, *"C'est qu'elle retourne vers sa source."* (In English: "It is returning to its source.")[142]

• Fritz Reiner was the conductor for an orchestra on a long American tour for which the program consisted of either Claude Debussy's *La Mer* or Richard Strauss' *Don Juan*. At one concert, a musician got mixed up and started playing *Don Juan* as the rest of the orchestra began to play *La Mer*. After the concert was over, Mr. Reiner told the musician that he was fired. The musician pleaded with him, saying that he had made a mistake that anyone could make in the midst of a long exhausting tour. Mr. Reiner replied, "Oh, it's not that — it's the way you play *Don Juan*."[143]

• Gioacchino Rossini was not fond of the sound of the high notes sung by the tenors of his day, and when Enrico Tamberlik wanted to visit him in Paris, Mr. Rossini requested that he leave his C-sharp in the vestibule until his visit was over.[144]

• Sir Thomas Beecham seemed by some to want to monopolize opera in Great Britain — something not appreciated by other British conductors. Sir Hamilton Harty once said, "British opera is dying slowly but surely — of TB."[145]

• Mikhail Ivanovich Glinka's opera *Russlan and Ludmilla* was a failure. In fact, it inspired the grand duke Mikhail Pavlovich to come up with a unique method of punishment — he forced offending officers to sit through the opera.[146]

• Not all tenors look impressive. When the diminutive 19th-century tenor Gilbert-Louis Duprez appeared in the dress rehearsal for his first *William Tell* in Paris, a ballet girl saw him and shouted, "What! That toad! Impossible!"[147]

• In the 20th century, sopranos Maria Callas and Renata Tebaldi feuded. Ms. Callas, however, denied that they were rivals: "How could we be rivals? I am champagne, and she is Coca-Cola."[148]

Kisses

• When Renata Tebaldi received her first kiss, she was disappointed. Her biographer, Victor Seroff, asked if the disappointment stemmed from the youth and inexperience of the man kissing her. She replied, "Too young and inexperienced at twenty-five? Not in Italy." (Fortunately, the second time he kissed her, she liked it.)[149]

• Conductor Arturo Toscanini was unhappy at a performance of Giuseppe Verdi's *Falstaff* — in one scene, the singers were not kissing in time to the music. Therefore, he demonstrated the correct way to kiss the soprano with a rapid series of kisses. "Like this!" he shouted. Eventually, the two singers kissed correctly.[150]

Chapter 4: From Language to Mothers

Language

• During World War I, opera singer Ernestine Schumann-Heink was requested to sing "The Star-Spangled Banner" for the American troops. Because she was so eager to help, she agreed, although she did not know the words. (She sang the tune, rather than the words, of the song.) Later, she read this comment in a newspaper article: "The voice of Schumann-Heink is a great inspiration when she sings 'The Star-Spangled Banner,' but we would be very obliged if she would tell us in what language she sings it." (Quickly thereafter, she learned the words.)[151]

• Very early in his career, Russian bass Feodor Chaliapine got work in the chorus of the French Light Opera Company. Very few of the members of the company were French, and the others did not know French. Fortunately, the members of the Russian audience also did not know French, thus allowing the singers to sing all the foreign words they knew at random — for example, "Colorado, Niagara, Mississippi, Charpentier, and Eau-de-vie ...."[152]

• Because of a lack of knowledge of English, Italian soprano Renata Tebaldi misunderstood what would happen when she agreed to sing Tosca in New York as a benefit for the Milk Fund. Speaking to a reporter, she expressed her opinion that "babies" would enjoy hearing this very emotional opera, and she was surprised to learn that the "babies" would not be attending the benefit.[153]

• French-born soprano Lily Pons learned her first American slang from comedian Jack Oakie — "Scram!" According to Mr. Oakie, Ms. Pons was the Metropolitan Opera's "Top Line Canary."[154]

Media

• Chicago Symphony Orchestra flutist Donald Peck was mightily unimpressed by opera singer Maria Callas. Once, the CSO was supposed to record with her. A rehearsal was scheduled, but Ms. Callas did not show up. The CSO waited for her because they were being paid for the time of the rehearsal, and when the rehearsal time was over they stood up to leave. At that exact time, Ms. Callas walked into the rehearsal space. Her agent made sure that the press knew that the CSO had risen out of respect to Ms. Callas, but Mr. Peck writes, "What a manipulation of the truth!"[155]

• Today, many people are amused by sensational stories in the tabloids; however, sensational stories are nothing new in American journalism. Once, several Philadelphia newspapers reported that soprano Adelina Patti had been devoured by mice. Here's what had really happened: In the early 1880s, hotels were not as sanitary as they are now. Ms. Patti, a tremendously wealthy woman, had rented an expensive apartment in a Philadelphia hotel. When her maid turned down the bedcovers, six mice jumped out. Later that night, a mouse bit the celebrated opera singer's left ear.[156]

Mishaps

• Opera singer Nellie Melba once toured the back-blocks — the remotest part of Australia. In one town, her concert was sold out. Some of the leading citizens neglected to buy tickets, thinking that they had discovered a way to hear Ms. Melba's concert for free. They used a ladder at the back of the hall to climb to the roof of the concert hall, where indeed they heard the concert for free. Unfortunately, the gardener discovered the ladder leading against the wall. Not wanting anyone to steal the ladder, he removed it and locked it up. After the concert, the town's leading free-loaders waited for everyone to leave, and then they discovered that they were stuck on the roof. Fortunately, about 5 a.m. a police officer happened by and rescued them. Ms. Melba wrote in her autobiography, *Melodies and Memories*, "I can well believe that that policeman lived comfortably on blackmail for the rest of his life." Another incident in the back-blocks involved a bill for some furniture. In honor of Ms. Melba, the hotel landlady ordered some fine furniture, which touched Ms. Melba. However, Ms. Melba was surprised to find the cost of the furniture added to her bill. Fortunately, her manager, John Lemmone, handled the situation. He said to the hotel landlady, "We shall be delighted to pay for the furniture, only of course if we do that, we shall take it away with us." The hotel landlady replied, "But I want it myself." Eventually, the hotel landlady concluded that if she wanted to keep the furniture she would have to pay for it.[157]

• Very early in his career, in the late 1920s in Italy, tenor Joseph Benton, aka Giuseppe Bentonelli, had costumes made up for the part of Faust. He had his housekeeper sew buttons on each pair of tights so he could use them for his suspenders. (He did notice that the housekeeper looked surprised at the request, but he didn't figure out why she looked surprised until he performed in the costume.) All went well during the performance — at first. Unfortunately, one suspender broke in two, and then the other suspender strap broke loose, too. Just as Faust took the lovely Marguerite in his arms at the conclusion of the opera, his tights fell down! The audience loved the mishap, and during the curtain calls the audience brought Mr. Benton back on stage for many bows. The headline in the local newspaper's review the next day stated, "FAUST TENOR LOSES PANTS ON STAGE." Following the debacle, Mr. Benton stopped using suspenders and learned how to tie his tights with bias tape so that they wouldn't fall down.[158]

• Early in her career, while making her first debuts on the operatic stage, Emma Calvé worried about her thin legs. Her mother didn't help, as she referred to them as "spider's legs." Therefore, while singing the role of Cherubin in *Noces de Figaro*, young Emma decided to do something about her thin legs and stuffed her tights with cotton so that she appeared to have calves instead of sticks. While singing, she was gratified to notice that the old gentlemen in the audience were looking at her calves through their opera glasses. However, during intermission the director told her, "What are those hideous lumps, I'd like to know!

I am tempted to stick pins into them! Stupid child! Don't you know that everyone is laughing at you? Do you expect anyone to believe that those fat excrescences belong to you! Take them off instantly!" In the second act, she appeared without enormous calves, a fact the audience noticed immediately and applauded uproariously.[159]

• While singing opera on a South American tour, Lucrezia Bori sometimes wore a dress that had a bell-shaped skirt. The bell shape of the skirt was created by a crinoline, which had to be tied tightly, for if it became undone the crinoline would raise the skirt much too high, thus revealing very much more than a lady wishes to reveal in public. Unfortunately, the fastening broke one day while Ms. Bori was singing on stage, the crinoline ballooned upward, carrying Ms. Bori's skirt with it, and a thoroughly embarrassed but thoroughly professional Ms. Bori continued to sing. Fortunately, Grassi, the tenor on stage, put a screen in front of Ms. Bori, and when Ms. Bori, still singing, came out from behind the screen, her skirt, now that she had removed the crinoline, was no longer bell-like and instead was modest.[160]

• In 1981, the Royal Opera House, Covent Garden, revived Verdi's *Un Ballo in Mashera.* Unfortunately, the opening night performance was marred. First, the scheduled tenor and baritone didn't show up, then the Amelia, performed by Montserrat Caballé, left the stage before her scene with Romeo. Because of the confusion, the stage curtain descended, and the conductor, Bernard Haitink, picked up the telephone in an effort to find out what was going on. When the switchboard operator answered, he said, "Haitink here. Give me the stage manager." The operator answered, "I'm sorry; I can't do that — there's a performance going on." Mr. Haitink looked at the stage curtain and said, "That's what you think."[161]

• Sometimes, high art is more disgusting than tabloid journalism. For example, in Richard Strauss' opera *Salome*, the severed head of John the Baptist is brought on a platter to the title character, who kisses its lips. At a 1978 production of this opera at Perth, Australia, a particularly gruesome head of the Baptist was created. It was to be brought out on stage, covered with a cloth. At the properly dramatic moment, Salome was to lift off the cloth, then shock the audience. At this particular production, however, a mistake was made. When Salome lifted off the cloth, the only thing to be seen on the platter was a stack of ham sandwiches.[162]

• In 1935, opera tenor Luciano Pavarotti was born in Modena, Italy, and his first critic was the doctor who delivered him. Hearing the infant scream, the doctor marveled, "Such high notes!" The ability to produce high notes under stress came in handy in 1969, when he was singing on stage in *La Bohème* in San Francisco when an earthquake struck. According to a 1979 article in *Time*, Pavarotti "gripped the hand of his Mimi, Dorothy Kirsten, a little more tightly, but kept on singing at full voice and never missed a beat. The earthquake drew to a peaceful conclusion and so did the performance."[163]

• Sir Rudolph Bing once said that opera singers do not fit easily into blue jeans. Soprano Rita Hunter once visited Disneyland, where she attempted to get through a turnstile leading out of Sleeping Beauty's Castle. Unfortunately, she got stuck. The day was hot, and as she and her family were waiting for a turnstile mechanic to arrive to help her, her daughter bought her an ice cream cone, then bought her another one. As Ms. Hunter was eating the second ice cream cone, she heard a Disney employee tell her daughter, "Jesus, sweetheart, don't feed her any more or we'll never get her out."[164]

• Franco Corelli used to carry around hidden sponges on stage while singing so he could occasionally wet his lips. Birgit Nilsson remembers that during the 1961 revival of *Turandot* at the Metropolitan Opera, Mr. Corelli suddenly turned his back on the audience, reached into the front of his pants, and, in Ms. Nilsson's words, "began fooling around." Of course, she was understandably worried about what he was going to do, and she was understandably relieved when he finally pulled out the sponge he had been searching for and wet his lips.[165]

• Long ago, women's underwear was held up by a button. While singing onstage in *La Bohème*, Frances Alda felt the button come loose and her pantalettes start falling down. Still singing, she stepped behind a sofa that was part of the scenery and let the underwear fall to the ground, then stepped out from behind the sofa. Unfortunately for Ms. Alda, tenor Enrico Caruso, who was on stage with her, saw what had happened, and he picked up the underwear and spread it out on the sofa for all the audience to see.[166]

• During theatrical events such as opera, backdrops are used to depict scenes. While Eugene Goossens was conducting *Die Götterdämmerung* in Liverpool, two backdrops were used. The bottom one showed a fire; the top one showed flames consuming the gods in Valhalla. Unfortunately, during a performance, only the top backdrop appeared — the lower backdrop showing the fire was missing, revealing this sign painted on the wall: NO SMOKING.[167]

• While Emma Albani was singing at a benefit night for herself at Covent Garden, an admirer threw a bouquet of flowers and a jewel case to her. Unfortunately, the jewel case struck her squarely on the forehead (greatly upsetting the gentleman who had thrown it), and Ms. Albani was forced to leave the stage. However, when she opened the jewel case and discovered that it contained a beautiful jewelled diadem, she was not angry with the gift giver.[168]

• The plot of an opera by Thea Musgrave revolves around a corpse in a bed on stage. In a 1961 production at the London Opera Centre, director Anthony Besch refused to let anyone other than himself handle the "corpse" that the props department had created, but at one performance, he forgot about it until the last moment. As the curtain opened, Mr. Besch was discovered running across the stage and carrying the corpse to the bed.[169]

• Conductor Sir Georg Solti once accidentally stabbed his hand with his baton and had to leave a performance because he was bleeding so much. Fortunately, the orchestra and singers performed well as the opera continued without him. By the way, Sir Georg once played a practical joke on a singer who did not know Hebrew. Just before a concert in Tel Aviv, Israel, he had a rabbi go over to the singer and thank him for agreeing to sing — in Hebrew.[170]

• During *Tosca*, a fire started on stage while Geraldine Farrar was performing. The prompter started to throw a fire extinguisher to Ms. Farrar, but she motioned to him not to do it. Instead, she acted shocked, then beat out the fire with her hands. Later, she explained that a modern fire extinguisher did not belong in *Tosca* and she preferred to injure her hands rather than to do violence to the opera.[171]

• While on tour in Manchester in the 1950s, the London Philharmonic Orchestra played in an orchestra pit that was so small that the musicians were forced to open the door under the stage so they would have room for the overflow. On stage, Radames called, "Aïda, where art thou?" Immediately afterward, from the door under the stage was heard the loud flushing of a toilet.[172]

• Tenor Ben Davies enjoyed telling about a performance of Mozart's *Don Giovanni* in which a very fat baritone played Don Giovanni. In the scene in which Don Giovanni descends into Hell, the baritone was supposed to go down below the stage through a trapdoor, but he was so fat that he got stuck. A member of the audience called out, "Hurrah, boys! Hell's full!"[173]

• At a performance of Wagner's *Lohengrin* at the Metropolitan Opera, tenor Leo Slezak was supposed to exit the stage in a swan-boat, but unfortunately, the swan-boat left before he was able to get in, leaving him stranded on stage like any ordinary person who has missed the bus. Mr. Slezak ad-libbed, "What time's the next swan?"[174]

• In 1916, a heavyweight bout held in the Manhattan Opera House in New York City featured Charley Weinert hitting Andre Anderson and knocking him through the ropes. Mr. Anderson fell into a pile of musical instruments and his rear end got stuck in the mouth of a tuba. As Mr. Anderson struggled to free himself, the referee counted to 10.[175]

• Herbert von Karajan sometimes did the lighting for the operas he conducted. Sir Rudolf Bing felt that frequently his lighting was murky, and after Mr. Karajan once told him that the lighting for a certain opera had required "eight full-length lighting rehearsals," Sir Rudolf replied, "I could have got it that dark with one."[176]

• Early in her career, Geraldine Farrar wrote Lilli Lehmann, asking to be permitted to become a pupil of hers. No reply came back, so her mother wrote Ms. Lehmann. A reply immediately came back — Ms. Lehmann explained that she had received Geraldine's letter, but she had been unable to read her handwriting.[177]

• During a performance of *Electra* with Birgit Nielsen at the Paris Opera, the lights went out due to a power failure. When the lights came on again, Richard Lewis picked up the performance where it had ended by singing his next lines: "Lights. Lights. Is there no one here to light them?"[178]

• Australian soprano Joan Sutherland, aka La Stupenda, enjoyed the music of Tchaikovsky, although for a while she liked his music less well than usual — as she was getting her teeth capped, her dentist played the music of Tchaikovsky in the background.[179]

• Sir John Gielgud was producing a Mozart opera at Covent Garden when something went wrong during a dress rehearsal. This upset Sir John, who shouted, "Oh, stop, stop, stop! Do stop that *dreadful* music!"[180]

Money

• Opera tenor Enrico Caruso became a coin collector through his old friend Mr. Amedeo Canessa. During a conversation, Mr. Canessa showed Mr. Caruso a gold coin on one side of which the head of Queen Arsinoë was engraved. Mr. Canessa said, "That little thing costs

500 francs." Mr. Caruso replied, "It's beautiful. I like it. But what is the use of one? I don't want one coin." Mr. Canessa said, "There is only this one. It is a very rare specimen." Mr. Caruso really liked the coin. He said, "Very well, then. It's mine." He then began to collect coins — more than 2,000 of them — as well as antique glass, bronzes, enamel, furniture, pottery, and watches. Mr. Caruso was generous with his wealth. A street cleaner — an elderly Italian — once saw him stopped on a street in a car. The old Italian shouted, "*Carus*!" Then he jumped on the car's running board. Enrico engaged in conversation with him in the Neapolitan dialect, and he shook his hand. As the old Italian turned to go, Enrico stuffed some money into one of his pockets.[181]

• Walter Damrosch hired Emil Fischer, bass from the Dresden Royal Opera, to sing at the Metropolitan Opera Company. Mr. Fischer made $250 per appearance, but he was not happy in his marriage and requested that his written contract state that he made $200 per appearance and that he receive the other $50 in cash. This was a way for him to hide about $600 per month from his wife so he could have some money of his own. His wife complained to Mr. Damrosch, "I do not know why my Emil is so badly paid while all the others get these enormous salaries. My Emil sings better than any of them, and he has to be content with only two hundred dollars an appearance!" Mr. Damrosch kept Mr. Fischer's secret.[182]

• Philip Crispano was a friend of the very popular opera tenor Enrico Caruso. Knowing that, an official of a town's Chamber of Commerce came to him and offered him $2,000 if he could convince Mr. Caruso to sing in the Chamber of Commerce's town. Mr. Crispano mentioned the offer to Mr. Caruso, who explained that his managers drew up his itinerary, and he had no idea if he would sing in that town. Mr. Caruso then added, "But look — you lose two thousand dollars because of this, don't you?" Mr. Caruso immediately wrote a check for

$2,000 and gave it to Mr. Crispano, who thanked him for it — then tore it up.[183]

• In his student days, basso Luigi Lablache once ran away from the conservatorium, signed a contract to sing at Salerno and received a month's salary in advance. However, he had a good time in Naples and spent all the money. He owned a portmanteau, but had nothing to fill it with. Aware that he could not appear in Salerno without luggage, he filled his portmanteau with sand and had it taken to Salerno. However, he was forced to return to the conservatorium. To recover the month's salary he had paid in advance, the impresario took possession of Mr. Lablache's portmanteau, but was disappointed with its contents.[184]

• An organ grinder once played music from Gioachino Rossini's *Barber of Seville* under the window of rival composer Fromental Halévy, who told him, "I will give you a Louis d'or if you go and play music from one of my operas under Rossini's windows." The organ grinder replied, "I cannot do that. Rossini has paid me two Louis d'or to play *his* music under *your* windows." By the way, some of Mr. Rossini's friends wanted to erect a statue of him. Told that the statue would cost approximately 20,000 lire, Mr. Rossini proposed, "Why don't you give me 10,000 lire, and I will stand on the pedestal myself?"[185]

• Vencenzo Lombardi greatly admired the tenor Enrico Caruso and early in Mr. Caruso's career told conductor Leopoldo Mugnone that soon the tenor would be making 1,000 lire a night. Mr. Mugnone disagreed: "Nonsense! When Enrico Caruso makes 1,000 lire a night, I'll be the pope!" Soon afterward, Mr. Caruso was making 1,000 lire a night, and Mr. Lombardi sought Mr. Mugnone. When he found him, Mr. Lombardi pretended to kneel and kiss the conductor's feet. Mr. Mugnone exclaimed, "What the h*ll!" Mr. Lombardi said to him, "Haven't you heard? Caruso is making 1,000 lire a night. You're the pope!"[186]

• Soprano Adelina Patti once lost her voice after two acts and was unable to finish the opera *Don Pasquale*. The director of the opera house was frantic, and having noticed another soprano, Madame Volpini, in the audience, he asked her to take over for Ms. Patti. Madame Volpini was no fool — she did take over, but at considerable advantage to herself. Her contract had not been renewed for the following year, but she managed to negotiate both a one-year contract and a raise of 5,000 francs before taking over for Ms. Patti.[187]

• Getting paid for your work can be quite a challenge. Impresario Alfredo Salmaggi once stepped in front of a curtain to announce to the audience that the scheduled performance of *Aida* had been cancelled because the tenor was indisposed. However, the tenor, Bernardo de Muro, immediately came in front of the curtain to make his own announcement: "I'm not indisposed! This b*stard won't pay me!" Lots of shouting ensued, but eventually Mr. de Muro got paid, and the performance went on as scheduled.[188]

• Opera singer Mary Garden was getting ready to sail to France when a young woman met her on the dock and asked, "Wouldn't you like a perfume called after your name?" Ms. Garden would, and she signed a paper the young woman gave her to sign. When she returned to the United States, she saw her name and face plastered everywhere advertising a perfume called "Mary Garden," and because of the paper she had signed, she never received a cent from the sales of the perfume.[189]

• At a Verdi festival, both Arturo Toscanini and a rival conductor were asked to conduct. The rival conductor was jealous of Maestro Toscanini's abilities, so he asked the organizers of the festival to pay him one lira more than Maestro Toscanini received. The organizers agreed, and after the festival was over, they gave the rival conductor a check for one lira. (Maestro Toscanini had donated his services.)[190]

• According to Lotte Lehmann, in Vienna the singer playing the role of the elder Des Grieux in *Manon* used to have a running joke whenever he named the sum that the younger Des Grieux would receive as an inheritance. Sometimes the amount would be pitifully small; at other times it would be extravagant. This is something that singers on stage looked forward to hearing, and musicians in the orchestra made bets about the amount.[191]

• In Vienna, while rehearsing *Tristan*, Birgit Nilsson suffered the misfortune of having her pearl necklace break. Everyone present helped her pick up the pearls. Pausing briefly, conductor Herbert von Karajan asked her, "Tell me, is this stage jewelry, or are they real pearls bought from your phenomenal Scala fees?" Ms. Nilsson replied, "Oh, no. These are cheap and ordinary pearls bought from your Vienna fees."[192]

• After Dame Nellie Melba was given a worthless check for an opera performance, she insisted on being paid in cash. In fact, she refused to go on stage until her money had been counted out in her presence, the money placed in a trunk in her dressing room, her maid seated on the trunk, and the dressing room door securely locked until after her performance.[193]

• In 1916, soprano Eva Turner started singing in the chorus of the Carl Rosa Opera Company. Soon, she started playing small parts. As the Page in *Tannhauser*, she earned an extra half-crown, which she put in the waistband of the baggy tights she wore as part of her costume and twisted so that the tights would not fall down.[194]

• Adelina Patti was well paid; in fact, she earned in one evening as much as the then-President of the United States earned in one year. When this was pointed out to her, she was not apologetic, instead replying, "Let him sing."[195]

• Wagner soprano Birgit Nilsson had a sense of humor. She once claimed Metropolitan Opera General Manager Rudolf Bing as a dependent on her income tax form.[196]

Mothers

• Opera singer Teresa Stratas, perhaps most famous for her performances in and recording of Alban Berg's *Lulu*, has a lot of respect for her mother: "She ran the house. She organized us for school. She washed our clothes — in those days, they used scrub boards — and she worked in the restaurant day and night and in between. She worked all hours. I don't ever remember her going to sleep and I don't remember her sitting down and eating a complete meal and not saying, 'Oh, I feel full — why don't you have the rest?'" When Nick, Teresa's brother, was older, some women came into the restaurant and talked to Nick and Teresa's mother. They said that Nick was old enough to quit school and go to work and do something for his mother — like buy jewelry for her. Nick and Teresa's mother then said something wise and wonderful: "My children are my jewelry."[197]

• When soprano Beverly Sills was pregnant with her second child, she received a telephone call from Sarah Caldwell asking her to play Rosalinda in a production of *Die Fledermaus* with conductor Arthur Fiedler. Ms. Sills was so excited by the offer that she immediately said yes. But when she hung up the telephone and told her husband, he asked her, "What are you planning to wear?" She replied, "Costumes," and then looked at her pregnant belly and realized what her husband meant. She immediately telephoned Ms. Caldwell and told her, "Miss Caldwell, I'm terribly sorry but I can't do your *Fledermaus* because I'm pregnant." Ms. Caldwell paused and then asked, "Weren't you pregnant five minutes ago?" By the way, Ms. Sills got her nickname — Bubbles — because when she was born, she had a huge bubble of saliva on her mouth.[198]

• This anecdote is not funny, but it does show the love a mother has for her child. During World War II, German soprano Elizabeth Schumann raised money for the Allies, but her son was a pilot for the Nazis. In 1945, while she was in London, she learned that during the Sicilian campaign her son had lost a leg after his plane was shot down. Being a mother, she wanted to help her son, even if he was on the wrong side in the war, so she tried to enlist the help of a friend in getting a well-made prosthesis to her son. The friend — who was bitter because of the many deaths that had occurred due to the Nazi bombing of London — replied that since her son had fought for Hitler, he would not help him. Ms. Schumann never again spoke to the former friend.[199]

• Adelina Patti's mother was willing to use underhanded methods to help her to succeed. Once, Ms. Patti was singing with a rival who had shaved her real eyebrows and put on false eyebrows. Ms. Patti's mother wanted to make the rival look ridiculous, so she began to stare at the rival. Under her breath, the rival asked, "What is the matter?" Ms. Patti's mother lied, "Your right eyebrow has fallen off!" Immediately, the rival tore off her left eyebrow and for the rest of the act wore only a right eyebrow.[200]

• In 1964, in West Berlin, Sarah Caldwell and her mother attended the premiere of *Montezuma*, an opera by Roger Sessions. Unfortunately, after the opera, the production people were booed. One of the people doing the booing was a man sitting next to Sarah's mother. Her mother was so angry at the man that she hit him with her fists. In 1976, Sarah presented the American premiere of the opera. Mr. Sessions heard the story about Sarah's mother and enjoyed repeating it to others.[201]

Chapter 5: From Parties to Work

Parties

• Italian soprano Claudia Muzio was known for keeping to herself, especially early in her career. She used to arrive at a theater for rehearsals, go directly to her dressing room and stay there until it was time to rehearse, and then disappear from the theater after the rehearsal without speaking to anyone. She also declined to go to most parties, saying, "I love my art and I permit nothing to interfere to its disadvantage. I can't understand how singers can go to suppers and dinners and receptions and still keep in good trim for their work." She and her mother often ate in hotel dining rooms — in a far corner — and didn't even nod to acquaintances who walked into the dining room.[202]

• Mid-1950s Metropolitan Opera basso Giorgio Tozzi and his wife once looked for a quiet apartment in Milan, Italy. He investigated an apartment, found it both charming and inexpensive, then looked around the streets, which were totally empty. Thinking that he had found the perfect place, he leased it. That night, around 10 p.m., the streets began to fill with people, and shouts, laughter, and other noises filled the air. No wonder the apartment had been so quiet in the middle of the afternoon — everyone was sleeping, for the apartment was located in the middle of the Milanese night life, which did not start until 10 p.m. and lasted all night![203]

• Opera soprano Marilyn Horne tells this story about composers: At a soiree, the hostess gave two composers — Gioachino Rossini and Gaetano Donizelli — a piece of paper each and asked them to write some music. Both wrote a beautiful melody, and when the hostess compared the two pieces of paper, she discovered that they had written the same beautiful melody. She told them, "Two creative talents can arrive at the same result!" But Donizelli replied, "Oh, no. We both stole it from Vincenzo Bellini."[204]

• As a famous opera singer, Geraldine Farrar had her share of invitations to parties just so she could provide entertainment. At one such party, the hostess requested of her, "Dear little songbird, do please sing that heavenly *Butterfly* entrance, I so seldom hear it." Ms. Farrar replied, "I am so sorry, but if you would arrive in your box before the middle of the first act, and stop chattering, you would hear it, in the opera house, where it belongs."[205]

Practical Jokes

• Comic singer Anna Russell, who was born British, became a naturalized American citizen. She was very nervous about taking her citizenship test, despite having studied for months. (Studying history was rather odd. In English schools, she had studied the War of Independence and learned that the Americans were the bad guys and the English were the good guys, but now she had to learn it the other way around.) An American official made her even more nervous when he looked at her ominously and said that he hoped she had studied hard. The official asked her to write a sentence in English, and then he asked her who was the first President of the United States. Finally, he signed her citizenship papers. A shocked Ms. Russell asked, "Is that all?" The American official replied, "Yes, but I had you rattled there, didn't I?"[206]

• Enrico Caruso was quite a practical joker off stage and on. Nellie Melba used to chew evergreen gum from Australia to keep her throat moist, chewing it before going on stage and then depositing it in a cup in the wings where she could use it to moisten her throat when she was once more off stage. Mr. Caruso once substituted chewing tobacco for the gum when Ms. Melba was on stage. On another occasion, in the last act of *La Bohème*, Ms. Melba, who was performing the role of the dying Mimi, was carefully lifted and placed on a bed. However, when the sheets of the bed were lifted so Mimi could be covered, the audience laughed — under the bed Mr. Caruso had ordered a stagehand to place a large object: a chamberpot.[207]

• Gerald Hoffnung often arranged a musical joke at his Hoffnung Festivals in London. On one occasion, Mr. Hoffnung announced to the audience that Sir William Walton had agreed to conduct an excerpt from his opera *Belshazzar's Feast*. Sir William came out on stage, along with soloist Owen Brannigan. Sir William raised his baton, and the members of the chorus sang out one word from the opera — "Slain!" Sir William then lowered his baton, shook hands with the soloist, and they left the stage — to appreciative applause from an audience who had enjoyed the joke.[208]

• Operatic bass singer Luigi Lablache was a huge man. One day, he was in Paris at the same time as the famous little person known as Tom Thumb. A lady wished to see the little person, but she mistakenly knocked at Mr. Lablache's door. Mr. Lablache opened the door, and the lady told him that she wished to see Tom Thumb. Mr. Lablache replied, "I am he." The lady expressed surprise, saying, "But I thought you were quite small!" Mr. Lablache replied, "So I am, madam, when I am on exhibition, but when I am at home, I always make myself comfortable."[209]

• Tenor Lauritz Melchior did his best to make soprano Helen Traubel laugh on stage. Sometimes, as she was singing an industrial-strength tragic aria, he would mutter to her, "For God's sake, Helena, hurry it up! I'm hungry and I need a beer!" In addition, when Ms. Traubel was onstage singing a tragic aria, Mr. Melchior would sometimes be in the wings dancing a hula while wearing a grass skirt and paper flowers, trying to make her laugh. Or he would wear a derby and a bearskin while dancing a Highland fling.[210]

• Heinrich Knote, a leading German tenor, once played a practical joke on Jean de Reszke. In Paris, Mr. Knote pretended to be a peddler and found an excuse to sing before Mr. de Reszke, who was very impressed and told him, "Sir, I engage you at once for the Opéra. You have gold in your throat." Mr. Knote later wrote a friend, "The incident was really most droll, and it cost me a terrific effort to play my role to the end without laughing."[211]

• In a performance of *Tosca*, Maria Jeritza decided to play a practical joke in her final scene, in which she stabbed the villain of the opera with a knife. On this particular night, instead of using a stage knife, she used a very ripe banana.[212]

Presidents, United States

• President Dwight David Eisenhower once attended a Metropolitan Opera production of *La Bohème*, at which the Secret Service did their duty, checking out anything that might possibly lead to an attempt on the President's life. One of the Secret Service men asked Met general manager Sir Rudolf Bing about the heroine of the opera, "We hear the girl dies. How is she killed?" Sir Rudolf replied, "She dies of consumption. It isn't contagious at a distance."[213]

• American opera star Jan Peerce had a meeting with President Harry S. Truman, but first he stopped to say the traditional prayers for his deceased parents in a synagogue. Arriving late for the meeting, he explained why he was late. President Truman replied, "I don't mind. The Lord won."[214]

Problem-Solving

• While singing Alfredo in *La Traviata* in Toronto, Canada, tenor John Brecknock had a Violetta who was rather standoffish and whose common comment in rehearsal was "Don't touch me." Mr. Brecknock, however, felt that in the love duet Alfredo and Violetta ought to be standing together, not apart, and he felt that Alfredo's arms should be around Violetta. Fortunately, he found a way to sing the love duet his way during the actual performance. Violetta wore a dress with a long train, and Alfredo simply stepped on the train, preventing Violetta from moving away from him. Alfredo then enclosed Violetta in his arms, and they sang the love duet together.[215]

• Guiseppe Verdi once stayed in a cottage at an Italian summer resort. A friend visited him and noticed that he seemed to be using only one room in the cottage. Curious, the friend asked him why he was not using the other rooms. Mr. Verdi showed him the other rooms, which were filled with 95 barrel organs. He explained, "All of these organs were playing *Rigoleto*, *Il Trovatore*, and other operas of mine. Obviously, I could not work under such circumstances. I decided to hire [rent] the organs from their owners. It will cost me about 1,500 lire for the summer, but it is not too large a price for a peaceful vacation."[216]

• While Italian soprano Luisa Tetrazzini was living in Argentina, where she was very popular, the 20-year-old son of her host fell in love with her. He appeared before her, holding a silver-handled dagger and threatening to kill himself if she did not kiss him. She replied, "We Italians never kiss anyone unless we know them very well. Now suppose you give me that lovely dagger of yours, then I will go out on the lawn and tell you presently if I like you well enough to kiss you." Her playing for time worked. She did not have to give the young man a kiss, but she did acquire a silver-handled dagger that she used for the next 15 years while singing Lucia di Lammermoor.[217]

• Marianne Brandt, an Austrian contralto, sang at the Metropolitan Opera House. She once went to the General Post Office at City Hall in New York City to receive a registered letter. The postal worker asked her for identification such as a passport, but she had none with her. The postal worker said, "I am sorry, madame, but the rules are strict." She replied, "You will not give me the letter? I will prove to you that I am Marianne Brandt!" She then loudly sang the cadenza from an aria in the opera *Le Prophète* by Giacomo Meyerbeer. The postal worker said, "Here is your letter, but for God's sake be quiet!"[218]

• During a visit with Sir Hugh Walpole by Mr. and Mrs. Lauritz Melchior, Mrs. Melchior had to use the bathroom, did, and discovered too late that no toilet paper was present. Seeing some other paper present in the form of books, she selected the least impressive volume and employed a few pages for a purpose they were not intended. Later, she discovered that Sir Hugh kept a number of priceless first editions in his bathroom, where he employed his sitting-down time perusing his collection.[219]

• Roger Prout used to help produce operas for the Welsh National Opera Company. One problem that concerned him was the breakage of glass props such as champagne glasses as the company moved from town to town. Writing "Fragile — Handle with Care" on the box didn't work, so he looked up the chemical formula for glass, then wrote "Na2 SiO3/Ca Si O3 — Handle with Extreme Care — Do Not Smoke" on the box. The breakage problem stopped immediately.[220]

• Like many famous people, coloratura soprano Lily Pons had a problem with people who too strongly insisted that she dine at their home, even when she needed to rest. To combat these "hosts," Ms. Pons would say that she would sup with them only if she could choose the menu. She then would choose a menu that was extremely difficult to prepare: steak châteaubriand, an exotic salad dressing, a rare wine, etc. Almost always, this solved the problem.[221]

• American soprano Grace Moore allowed no one to upstage her. Singing Mimi, she appeared with Jan Kiepura as Rodolfo. When Ms. Moore started singing *Me chiamano Mimi*," Mr. Kiepura moved to a position that partially blocked the audience's view of her. The people in the audience, including Lanfranco Rasponi, author of *The Last Prima Donnas*, long remembered how Ms. Moore shoved Mr. Kiepura aside — forcefully.[222]

• While soprano Emma Albani was singing in San Francisco, a problem developed when opera fans started sneaking into the theater through a window rather than buying tickets. To solve the problem, a police officer was stationed at the window. Unfortunately, whenever someone tried to climb through the window, the police officer forced him to pay a fee — which the police officer then put into his own pocket.[223]

• Sir Rudolf Bing once invited Maria Callas to sing the role of the Queen of the Night in Mozart's *Magic Flute*. She demurred, pointing out, "It doesn't make sense for you to pay such a large fee for such a small part." Sir Rudolf replied, "I have the solution! Reduce your fee."[224]

Recordings

• Very early in his career, John McCormack made a record titled "Killarney" for The Gramophone Company. Later, when he was a very famous opera singer, Mr. McCormack would play the record for distinguished visitors, saying that the recording was of a singer who wanted his advice about whether he ought to pursue singing professionally. Mr. McCormack said, "Without exception, everyone of them, including such an excellent critic as my friend Dr. Walter Starke, said, 'Oh, Lord, John, don't advise that poor boy to study singing. It is too pathetic for words.'" Then Mr. McCormack would show the listeners his name on the record and laugh and laugh. By the way, one of Mr. McCormack's funniest reviews appeared in the *Melbourne Australian* after he gave his first-ever concert at Exhibition Hall: "If this Irish boy is not known in a very few years as one of the greatest tenors in the world, it will probably be because a careless builder dropped a warehouse or a terrace on him as he was passing."[225]

• While recording an album, all involved must be very careful not to record extraneous noises such as squeaks. While recording the album *Diva!*, soprano Leslie Garrett and the musicians ran into a problem because of a squeak that would not go away. Thinking the squeak might come from a wobbly music stand, the musicians moved the music stands a few inches and tried again. The squeak remained. Thinking the squeak might come from a wobbly chair, the musicians moved the chairs a few inches and tried again. The squeak remained. Then Ms. Garrett took thought, held the music engineer's head to her chest, and asked, "Is that what you heard?" It was — the squeak came from the underwiring of her bra. Ms. Garrett removed her bra in the ladies room, then made a squeak-free recording. Afterward, whenever they recorded a new album together, the music engineer asked her, "Have you got the right bra on?"[226]

• Tenor Hugues Cuenod sang a very long piece on a recording of works by Francois Couperin. Igor Stravinsky heard and enjoyed the recording, so he asked Mr. Cuenod to sing his *Cantate*. However, Mr. Cuenod knew that the tenor would have to sing a 13-minute aria with no pauses, so he declined. Mr. Stravinsky complained, "But you sing 22 minutes without stopping in your Couperin recording; then why can't you sing 13 minutes of my music?" However, Mr. Cuenod says, "He had forgotten that it is possible to stop, start, and splice in making a recording, or even to do it in several takes; but that's obviously what I couldn't do in a live performance."[227]

Religion

• In the early 1900s, the Metropolitan Opera's production of *Parsifal* was considered scandalous — clergymen felt it was improper for a theater to stage religious drama. However, very quickly the scandal was forgotten and many theater-goers looked forward to seeing *Parsifal* annually on Good Friday.[228]

• In the late 19th century in Milan, a reporter heard someone playing the piano at 7 a.m., so he asked a member of the hotel staff if piano playing was allowed at such an early hour. The hotel staffer replied, "Not as a rule, but we make an exception for Verdi."[229]

Revenge

• Moravian soprano Maria Jeritza made enemies of many of the tenors with whom she sang. One such tenor, the Englishman Alfred Piccaver, decided to get even during a May 19, 1925, performance of *Cavalleria Rusticana* at the State Opera in Vienna, Austria. At the moment in which the Turiddu was supposed to push her character down the stairs, Mr. Piccaver simply stood with his arms crossed, and Ms. Jeritza had to throw herself down the stairs. Afterward, Ms. Jeritza refused to take a bow with Mr. Piccaver, and she became furious when he received more applause than she when they took their bows separately. For several months, she refused to sing with him, but within a year they stood on stage together as Tosca and Cavaradossi.[230]

• Early in soprano Joan Hammond's career in Australia, she was a member of the chorus in *I Pagliacci*, where she quickly discovered that some of the extras wanted to be front and center so their friends could see them. These "Footlight Fannies," and Ms. Hammond and her chorus-member friends called them, were unpopular, and Joan and her friends figured out a novel way to get revenge on these people. In one scene, the extras and chorus members sat on benches, and the Footlight Fannies, of course, ran and sat on the ends of the benches closest to the audience. Joan and her friends were also sitting on the benches, and at a prearranged signal, they suddenly stood up, letting the Footlight Fannies crash to the floor.[231]

Royalty

• The myth of the Judgment of Paris explains the origin of the Trojan War. The Trojan prince Paris was the judge of a heavenly beauty contest, in which he was to award a golden apple to the most beautiful goddess. He gave the golden apple to Venus, who helped him win the heart of Helen. Unfortunately, Helen was married, and the Trojan War was his attempt to get her back. An opera based on the myth — *Opera Il Pomo D'oro* — was presented when Leopold I married the Spanish princess Margarita in 1667. Antonio Cesti, the writer of the opera, was no fool — he made sure that the golden apple was given to Margarita.[232]

• Soprano Adelina Patti was beloved by royalty all over the world. Once, she was asked who was her favorite royal personage. She thought for a moment, and then answered, "Well, the Tsar Alexander gives the best jewelry."[233]

Sex

• Young, pretty opera singer Mary Garden was dining with an old man named Chauncey Depew, who was the President of the New

York Central Railroad. Ms. Garden was wearing a low-cut, shoulderless dress, and Mr. Depew kept staring at her cleavage. Finally, Mr. Depew asked, "I am wondering, Miss Garden, what keeps that dress up?" Ms. Garden replied, "Two things, Mr. Depew. Your age, and my discretion."[234]

• Sir Thomas Beecham once told a soprano, who was lying in a prone position during a death scene, to sing louder because he couldn't hear her. She replied, "Don't you realize that one can't give of one's best when one is in a prone position?" Sir Thomas replied, "I seem to recollect that I have given some of my best performances in that position."[235]

Superstitions

• Luciano Pavarotti had a superstition — he wouldn't sing unless he finds a bent, rusty nail on stage. Of course, smart opera impresarios make sure that their stage has a bent, rusty nail for Mr. Pavarotti to find. In New York, Mr. Pavarotti did not find a bent, rusty nail on stage, so he declined to sing. Fortunately, Maria Teresa Maschio also is superstitious, and she carries a bent, rusty nail for good luck. The theater personnel borrowed the bent, rusty nail, placed it on stage, Mr. Pavarotti found it, and the performance was saved — afterward, Ms. Maschio was given back her bent, rusty nail.[236]

• Many people in opera have either superstitions or little rituals that they perform, or both. After a performance, tenor Plácido Domingo will return to the empty stage and say *"Au revoir."* He regards this as a way of ensuring that he will return. And, like tenor Luciano Pavarotti, Mr. Domingo must find a bent nail before the performance. (Stagehands often plant bent nails for these tenors to find.)[237]

Tobacco

• Enrico Caruso smoked, and he insisted on smoking. While at the Imperial Theater of Berlin, he started smoking in his dressing room. The stage director visited him to tell him that no smoking was allowed in the theater. Mr. Caruso replied that he needed to smoke in order to calm his nerves. The stage director left him, but soon the opera superintendent visited him to tell him that no smoking was allowed in the theater. Mr. Caruso replied, "Dear sir, I regret infinitely, but I have already said that I feel very nervous, and if I am not allowed to smoke in peace, to my great regret I will not sing this evening." The superintendent suggested a compromise: Mr. Caruso could smoke as long as a fireman was in the dressing room with him. Mr. Caruso agreed to the compromise, and as he finished each cigarette the fireman took the butt from him and threw it in a bucket of water.[238]

• While singing Don Ottavio in *Don Giovanni* at the Teatro Colón, Buenos Aires, Argentina, tenor John Brecknock was invited to a dinner party, where he noticed that the guests frequently disappeared for a short time, then reappeared. Because he was a guest, he did not ask the reason for such behavior. Eventually, he asked for permission to smoke a cigar, and he discovered that the guests had been disappearing because they were desperate for a smoke, and they had assumed that they should not smoke around Mr. Brecknock because he was a singer.[239]

Weight

• Opera tenor Luciana Pavarotti made an unsuccessful movie titled *Yes, Giorgio*. Perhaps it was unsuccessful because Mr. Pavarotti was known for his voice (and his weight), not for his acting. According to Hollywood lore, Kate Jackson of *Charlie's Angels* fame almost signed up to co-star with Mr. Pavarotti, but singer/actress Cher advised her, "Never, never, *ever* do a movie where you can't get your arms around your romantic lead."[240]

• Tenor Luciano Pavarotti became quite fat late in his career, and people sometimes would ask him what he weighed. His usual reply was, "Less than before." Occasionally, people would want to know what his "before" weight had been. Mr. Pavarotti would then reply, "More than now."[241]

• Jimmy Dorsey was a fabulous jazz musician but not always very good at communicating orally. On Bing Crosby's radio show, Mr. Dorsey once introduced an overweight opera star in this way: "And now we bring you that great opera steer ...."[242]

Work

• When Sarah Caldwell began working at Tanglewood, a music venue in Massachusetts, she worked very hard because she was afraid that she might be fired (and because she always worked hard). One opera set designer had been fired because he had not given 200 percent — his sets were not finished on time. Ms. Caldwell did not want that to happen to her. In fact, she worked such long hours that she did not have time to attend the Tanglewood concerts. This worried her because rumor had it that the bigwigs kept track of who attended concerts and who did not. In fact, when Ms. Caldwell attended her first concert, the biggest wig of all, Serge Koussevitzky, said to her, "Caldwell, how nice to see you at a concert!" She worried about this, and she attended a second concert, and Dr. Koussevitzky said to her, "So, Caldwell, you have come to another concert!" A little later, she said to him, "Dr. Koussevitzky, there is just one thing wrong with Tanglewood." She then explained that she did not know how she could give 200 percent and still find time to attend concerts. Dr. Koussevitzky hugged her and replied, "I never want to see you at another concert." By the way, when Ms. Caldwell began studying at the New England Conservatory of Music in Boston, Massachusetts, her father gave her some good advice. She wrote in her autobiography, "He suggested that I major in professors. He said that if I found a wonderful, brilliant professor, it wouldn't make any difference what he was teaching. I should learn from him, try to determine how his mind worked, what he considered important, how he behaved, and how he reacted."[243]

• Wolfgang Amadeus Mozart used to work for Hieronymus von Colloredo, an archbishop; however, they did not respect each other. The archbishop treated Mozart badly and did not pay him well; in return, Mozart called the archbishop an "archbooby." When Mozart's opera *Idomeneo* became a success in 1781, he decided to leave the archbishop's employ. They had a loud argument, and Mozart's employment ended. As a final humiliation, the archbishop's secretary kicked Mozart in the seat of his pants.[244]

• As a young singer, conductor Richard Tauber especially liked to sing the role of Narraboth in *Salome* because the character is killed 20 minutes into the opera, then dragged off stage. This meant that he could leave the theater early and catch the last showing of a movie if he wished. Unfortunately, during one performance, the guards forgot to drag him off stage, so he was forced to lie on the stage, breathing shallowly for an extra 90 minutes.[245]

• Sometimes, it doesn't pay to lie. Early in her career, to get a job in show business, Grace Moore decided to lie. Therefore, she went to the Packard Agency. When the manager asked Ms. Moore about her experience, she brazenly answered that she had been performing in the operetta *The Lilac Domino* on a West Coast tour. The manager looked her right in the eyes and said, "That ain't so, for that's our company."[246]

• As an immigrant in Paris, Henny Youngman's father made a living as a professional applauder for opera performers. Any opera singer who wanted to be sure of making a hit could hire as many professional applauders as he or she felt was needed to ensure being called back for an encore. (Some professional applauders also made money by specializing in crying at sad numbers or laughing at happy ones.)[247]

• Two of the giants of opera are tenors Plácido Domingo and Luciano Pavarotti. Mr. Domingo actually has a double career in music; he often conducts. One day, after Mr. Domingo had conducted a concert, he said to Mr. Pavarotti, "It's wonderful to have this double career. Why don't you try it, Luciano?" Mr. Pavarotti replied, "What, with a voice like mine?"[248]

• As a young man, English tenor Walter Midgley worked as a clerk at an iron and steel works, picking up extra money during his off-time by singing. He was so successful at this that he drove a better car than one of the directors, who wondered for a while if the young clerk might be getting his extra money through such extra-curricular activities as burglaries.[249]

• Musicians can get tired of playing the same music — even great music — over and over throughout an opera season. Critic Patrick J. Smith remembers seeing a musician at the end of a performance of *Götterdämmerung* lean over and kiss the last page of the score.[250]

Appendix A: Book Bibliography

Albani, Emma. *Forty Years of Song*. New York: Arno Press, 1977.

Alda, Frances. *Men, Women, and Tenors*. Boston, Massachusetts: Houghton Mifflin Company, 1937.

Anton Seidl: A Memorial by His Friends. New York: Charles Scribner's Sons, 1899.

Atkins, Harold and Archie Newman, compilers. *Beecham Stories*. Great Britain: Futura Publications Limited, 1978.

Ayre, Leslie. *The Wit of Music*. Boston, Massachusetts: Crescendo Publishing Company, 1969.

Barber, David W. *If It Ain't Baroque ...: More Music History as It Ought to be Taught*. Toronto, Canada: Sound and Vision, 1992.

Barber, David W. *When the Fat Lady Sings: Opera History as It Ought to be Taught*. Toronto, Canada: Sound and Vision, 1990.

Barthelemy, Richard. *Memories of Caruso*. Trans. Constance S. Camner. Plainsboro, New Jersey: La Scala Autographs, 1979.

Beach, Scott. *Musicdotes*. Berkeley, California: Ten Speed Press, 1977.

Bessette, Roland L. *Mario Lanza: Tenor in Exile*. Portland, Oregon: Amadeus Press, 1999.

Benton, Joseph. *Oklahoma Tenor: Musical Memories of Giuseppe Bentonelli*. Norman, Oklahoma: University of Oklahoma Press, 1973.

Bing, Sir Rudolf. *5000 Nights at the Opera*. Garden City, New York: Doubleday and Company, Inc., 1972.

Bing, Sir Rudolf. *A Knight at the Opera*. New York: G.P. Putnam's Sons, 1981.

Blackwood, Alan. *The Performing World of the Singer*. Morristown, New Jersey: Silver Burdett Company, 1981.

Blum, David. *Quintet: Five Journeys Toward Musical Fulfillment*. Ithaca, NY, and London: Cornell University Press, 1999.

Bocelli, Andrea. *The Music of Silence: A Memoir*. New York: HarperEntertainment, 1999.

Böhm, Karl. *A Life Remembered: Memoirs*. Trans. John Kehoe. London and New York: M. Boyars, 1992.

Bonvicini, Candido. *The Tenor's Son: My Days With Pavarotti*. New York: St. Martin's Press, 1992.

Borge, Victor, and Robert Sherman. *My Favorite Comedies in Music*. New York: Franklin Watts, 1980.

Borge, Victor. *My Favorite Intervals*. London: The Woburn Press, 1971.

Boyden, John, collector. *Stick to the Music: Scores of Orchestral Tales.* London: Souvenir Press, 1992.

Brecknock, John L., and John Kennedy Melling. *Scaling the High Cs: The Musical Life of Tenor John L. Brecknock.* Lanham, Maryland, and London: The Scarecrow Press, Inc., 1996.

Breslin, Herbert H., editor. *The Tenors.* New York: Macmillan Publishing Co., Inc., 1974.

Brook, Donald. *Singers of Today.* Freeport, New York: Books for Libraries Press, 1971.

Callas, Evangelia. *My Daughter Maria Callas.* New York: Fleet Publishing Corporation, 1960.

Caldwell, Sarah. *Challenges: A Memoir of My Life in Opera.* With Rebecca Matlock. Middleton, Connecticut: Wesleyan University Press, 2008.

Calvé, Emma. *My Life.* Trans. Rosamond Gilder. New York. Arno Press, 1977.

Cardus, Neville, editor. *Kathleen Ferrier: A Memoir.* London: Hamish Hamilton, Ltd., 1954.

Caruso, Dorothy. *Enrico Caruso: His Life and Death.* New York: Simon and Schuster, Inc., 1945.

Caruso, Dorothy, and Torrance Goddard. *Wings of Song: The Story of Caruso.* New York: Minton, Balch & Company, 1928.

Chaliapine, Feodor Ivanovitch. *Pages From My Life: An Autobiography.* Trans. H.M. Buck. New York and London: Harper and Brothers, Publishers, 1927.

Chapin, Schuyler. *Sopranos, Mezzos, Tenors, Bassos, and Other Friends.* New York: Crown Publishers, Inc., 1995.

Chotzinoff, Samuel. *Toscanini: An Intimate Portrait.* New York: Alfred A. Knopf, 1956.

Cortesi, Salvatore. *My Thirty Years of Friendships.* New York: Harper and Brothers, Publishers, 1927.

Cott, Ted. *The Victor Book of Musical Fun.* New York: Simon and Schuster, Inc., 1945.

Cranston, Toller. *Zero Tollerance.* With Martha Lowder Kimball. Toronto, Canada: McClelland and Stewart, Inc., 1997.

Crow, Bill. *Jazz Anecdotes.* New York: Oxford University Press, 1990.

Damrosch, Walter. *My Musical Life.* New York: Charles Scribner's Sons, 1923.

Domingo, Plácido. *My First Forty Years.* New York: Alfred A Knopf, 1983.

Douglas, Nigel. *Legendary Voices.* London: Andre Deutsch Limited, 1992.

Douglas, Nigel. *More Legendary Voices.* London: Andre Deutsch Limited, 1994.

Drake, James A, and Kristin Beall Ludecke, editors. *Lily Pons: A Centennial Portrait.* Portland, Oregon: Amadeus Press, 1999.

Epstein, Lawrence J. *A Treasury of Jewish Anecdotes*. Northvale, New Jersey: Jason Aronson, Inc., 1989.

Ewen, David. *Famous Conductors*. New York: Dodd, Mead & Company, 1966.

Ewen, David, complier. *Listen to the Mocking Words*. New York: Arco Publishing Co., 1945.

Farrar, Geraldine. *Geraldine Farrar: The Story of an American Singer*. Boston, Massachusetts, and New York: Houghton Mifflin Company, 1916.

Farrar, Geraldine. *Such Sweet Compulsion*. New York: The Greystone Press, 1938.

Feather, Leonard, and Jack Tracy. *Laughter from the Hip: The Lighter Side of Jazz*. New York: Da Capo Press, Inc., 1979.

Finck, Henry T. *Musical Laughs*. New York: Funk & Wagnalls Company, 1924.

Finck, Henry T. *My Adventures in the Golden Age of Music*. New York and London: Funk & Wagnalls Company, 1926.

Finletter, Gretchen. *From the Top of the Stairs*. Boston, Massachusetts: Little, Brown and Company, 1946.

Garden, Mary, and Louis Biancolli. *Mary Garden's Story*. New York: Simon and Schuster, Inc., 1951.

Garrett, Leslie. *Notes from a Small Soprano*. London: Hodder and Stoughton, 2000.

Greenfield, Edward. *Joan Sutherland*. New York: Drake Publishers, Inc., 1973.

Groover, David L., and Cecil C. Conner, Jr. *Skeletons from the Opera Closet*. New York: St. Martin's Press, 1986.

Guerilla Girls. *Bitches, Bimbos and Ballbreakers: The Guerilla Girls' Illustrated Guide to Female Stereotypes*. New York: Penguin Books, 2003.

Hammond, Joan. *A Voice, A Life*. London: Victor Gollancz Ltd., 1970.

Hewlett-Davies, Barry, editor and compiler. *A Night at the Opera*. New York: St. Martin's Press, 1980.

Heylbut, Rose, and Aimé Gerber. *Backstage at the Opera*. New York: Thomas Y. Crowell Company, 1937.

Horne, Marilyn. *Marilyn Horne: My Life*. With Jane Scovell. New York: Atheneum, 1983.

Hudry, Francois. *Hugues Cuenod: With a Nimble Voice*. Trans. Albert Fuller. Hillsdale, New York: Pendragon Press, 1998.

Huggett, Richard. *Supernatural on Stage: Ghosts and Superstitions of the Theatre*. New York: Taplinger Publishing Company, 1975.

Hunter, Rita. *Wait Till the Sun Shines, Nellie*. London: Hamish Hamilton Ltd., 1986.

Jadan, Doris. *The Great Life of Ivan Jadan*. St. John, Virgin Islands: Caribbean Booksmiths, 1995.

Jampol, Joshua. *Living Opera*. Oxford: Oxford University Press, 2010.

Jones, Millicent. *The World's Greatest Tenors*. North Dighton, Massachusetts: JG Press, 1995.

Kallen, Stuart A. *Great Composers*. San Diego, California: Lucent Books, 2000.

Karkar, Jack and Waltraud, compilers and editors. *... And They Danced On*. Wausau, Wisconsin: Aardvark Enterprises, 1989.

Kaufmann, Helen L. *Anecdotes of Music and Musicians*. New York: Grosset & Dunlap, Publishers, 1960.

Kesting, Jürgen. *Luciano Pavarotti: The Myth of the Tenor*. Trans. Susan H. Ray. Boston, Massachusetts: Northeastern University Press, 1991.

Lahee, Henry C. *Famous Singers of To-day and Yesterday*. Boston, Massachusetts: L.C. Page and Company, 1898.

Lauw, Louisa. *Fourteen Years with Adelina Patti*. La Scala Autographs, 1977.

Lawrence, Marjorie. *Interrupted Melody: The Story of My Life*. New York: Appleton-Century-Crofts, Inc., 1949.

Lawrence, Robert. *A Rage for Opera: Its Anatomy as Drawn from Life*. New York: Dodd, Mead and Company, 1971.

Lawton, Mary. *Schumann-Heink: The Last of the Titans*. New York: The Macmillan Company, 1928.

Ledbetter, Gordon T. *The Great Irish Tenor*. New York: Charles Scribner's Sons, 1977.

Lehmann, Lotte. *My Many Lives*. New York: Boosey and Hawkes, Inc., 1948.

Linkletter, Art. *I Wish I'd Said That! My Favorite Ad-Libs of All Time*. Garden City, New York: Doubleday & Co., Inc., 1968.

Mapleson, Colonel J.H. *The Mapleson Memoirs: The Career of an Operatic Impresario, 1858-1888*. Harold Rosenthal, ed. New York: Appleton-Century, 1966.

Marion, John Francis. *Lucrezia Bori of the Metropolitan Opera*. New York: P.J. Kenedy & Sons, 1962.

Matheopoulos, Helena. *The Great Tenors From Caruso to the Present*. New York: St. Martin's Press, 1999.

Matz, Mary Jane. *Opera Stars in the Sun: Intimate Glimpses of Metropolitan Personalities*. New York: Farrar, Straus, and Cudahy, 1955.

McArthur, Edwin. *Flagstad: A Personal Memoir*. New York: Alfred A. Knopf, 1965.

McCormack, Lily. *I Hear You Calling Me*. Milwaukee, Wisconsin: The Bruce Publishing Company, 1949.

Melba, Nellie. *Melodies and Memories*. New York: George H. Doran Company, 1926.

Monteux, Doris G. *It's All in the Music*. New York: Farrar, Straus and Giroux, 1965.

Moore, Gerald. *Am I Too Loud? Memoirs of an Accompanist*. London: Hamish Hamilton, 1979.

Moore, Grace. *You're Only Human Once*. Garden City, New York: Doubleday, Doran and Co., Inc., 1944.

Morley, Robert. *Robert Morley's Book of Bricks*. New York: G.P. Putnam's Sons, 1979.

Morrissey, James W. *Noted Men and Women*. New York: The Klebold Press, 1910.

Newman, Danny. *Tales of a Theatrical Guru*. Urbana and Chicago, Illinois: University of Illinois Press, 2006.

Oakie, Victoria Horne, compiler and editor. *"Dear Jack": Hollywood Birthday Reminiscences to Jack Oakie*. Portland, Oregon: Strawberry Hill Press, 1994.

O'Connell, Charles. *The Other Side of the Record*. New York: Alfred A. Knopf, 1949.

Opera Magazine Ltd. *Sopranos in Opera: Profiles of Fifteen Great Sopranos*. London: Opera Magazine Ltd., 2002.

Opera Magazine Ltd. *Tenors in Opera: Profiles of Fifteen Great Tenors*. London: Opera Magazine, Ltd., 2003.

Owen, H. Goddard. *A Recollection of Marcella Sembrich*. Bolton, New York: The Marcella Sembrich Memorial Association, Inc., 1950.

Paolucci, Bridget. *Beverly Sills*. New York: Chelsea House Publishers, 1990.

Pavarotti in Opera. London: Opera Magazine, Ltd., 2008.

Peck, Donald. *The Right Time, The Right Place! Tales of Chicago Symphony Days*. Bloomington and Indianapolis, Indiana: Indiana University Press, 2007.

Peltz, Mary Ellis. *The Magic of the Opera: A Picture Memoir of the Metropolitan*. New York: Frederick A. Praeger, Inc., 1960.

Pleasants, Henry. *The Great Singers: From the Dawn of Opera to Our Own Time*. New York: Simon and Schuster, 1966.

Pleasants, Henry, editor. *The Great Tenor Tragedy*. Portland, Oregon: Amadeus Press, 1995.

Rasky, Harry. *Stratas*. Toronto, New York: Oxford University Press, 1988.

Rasponi, Lanfranco. *The Last Prima Donnas*. New York: Alfred A. Knopf, 1984.

Rogers, Clara Kathleen (Clara Doria). *Memories of a Musical Career*. Norwood, Massachusetts: The Plimpton Press, 1932.

Rogers, Francis. *Some Famous Singers of the 19th Century*. New York: Arno Press, 1977.

Ross-Russell, Noel. *There Will I Sing*. London: Open Gate Press, 1996.

Rossi, Alfred. *Astonish Us in the Morning: Tyrone Guthrie Remembered.* London: Hutchinson & Co., Publishers, 1977.

Rubin, Stephen E. *The New Met in Profile.* New York: Macmillan Publishing Co., Inc., 1974.

Russell, Anna. *I'm Not Making This Up, You Know: The Autobiography of the Queen of Musical Parody.* New York: The Continuum Publishing Company, 1985.

Savage, Richard Temple. *A Voice from the Pit.* Newton Abbot; North Pomfret, Vermont: David & Charles, 1988.

Scherer, Barrymore Laurence. *Bravo! A Guide to Opera for the Perplexed.* New York: Dutton, 1996.

Schwarzkopf, Elisabeth. *On and Off the Record: A Memoir of Walter Legge.* New York: Charles Scribner's Sons, 1982.

Seroff, Victor. *Renata Tebaldi: The Woman and the Diva.* Freeport, New York: Books for Libraries Press, 1970.

Shear, Nancy. *The Three Tenors.* New York: MetroBooks, 1998.

Sills, Beverly. *Bubbles: A Self-Portrait.* Indianapolis, Indiana, and New York: Bobbs-Merrill, 1976.

Slezak, Leo. *Song of Motley.* New York: Arno Press, 1977.

Slezak, Walter. *What Time's the Next Swan?* Garden City, New York: Doubleday and Co., Inc., 1962.

Slonimsky, Nicolas. *Slonimsky's Book of Musical Anecdotes.* New York and London: Routledge, 2002.

Smith, H. Allen. *The Compleat Practical Joker.* Garden City, New York: Doubleday and Company, Inc., 1953.

Smith, Patrick J. *A Year at the Met.* New York: Alfred A. Knopf, 1983.

Sobol, Donald J. *Encyclopedia Brown's Book of Wacky Sports.* New York: William Morrow and Company, 1984.

Sorel, Nancy Caldwell, and Edward Sorel. *First Encounters: A Book of Memorable Meetings.* New York: Alfred A. Knopf, 1994.

Stefoff, Rebecca. *Plácido Domingo.* New York: Chelsea House Publishers, 1992.

Story, Rosalyn M. *And So I Sing: African-American Divas of Opera and Concert.* New York: Warner Books, 1990.

Tanner, Stephen. *Opera Antics and Anecdotes.* Toronto, Canada: Sound and Vision, 1999.

Traubel, Helen. *St. Louis Woman.* New York: Duell, Sloan and Pearce, 1959.

Turing, Penelope. *Hans Hotter, Man and Artist.* London: John Calder, 1983. Foreword by Sir Georg Solti.

Vickers, Hugh. *Even Greater Operatic Disasters.* New York: St. Martin's Press, 1982.

Vickers, Hugh. *Great Operatic Disasters*. New York: St. Martin's Press, Inc., 1979. Introduction by Sir Peter Ustinov.

Wagenknecht, Edward. *Seven Daughters of the Theater*. Norman, Oklahoma: University of Oklahoma Press, 1964.

Wagner, Alan. *Prima Donnas and Other Wild Beasts*. Larchmont, New York: Argonaut Books, 1961.

Wagnalls, Mabel. *Stars of the Opera*. New York: Funk & Wagnalls Company, 1906.

Wellman, Sam. *Mariah Carey*. Philadelphia, Pennsylvania: Chelsea House Publishers, 2000.

Williams, Kenneth. *Acid Drops*. London: J.M. Dent & Sons, Ltd., 1980.

Ybarra, T.R. *Caruso: The Man of Naples and the Voice of God*. New York: Harcourt, Brace and Company, 1953.

Youngman, Henny. *Take My Life, Please!* With Neal Karlen. New York: William Morris and Company, Inc., 1991.

Appendix B: About the Author

It was a dark and stormy night. Suddenly a cry rang out, and on a hot summer night in 1954, Josephine, wife of Carl Bruce, gave birth to a boy — me. Unfortunately, this young married couple allowed Reuben Saturday, Josephine's brother, to name their first-born. Reuben, aka "The Joker," decided that Bruce was a nice name, so he decided to name me Bruce Bruce. I have gone by my middle name — David — ever since.

Being named Bruce David Bruce hasn't been all bad. Bank tellers remember me very quickly, so I don't often have to show an ID. It can be fun in charades, also. When I was a counselor as a teenager at Camp Echoing Hills in Warsaw, Ohio, a fellow counselor gave the signs for "sounds like" and "two words," then she pointed to a bruise on her leg twice. Bruise Bruise? Oh yeah, Bruce Bruce is the answer!

Uncle Reuben, by the way, gave me a haircut when I was in kindergarten. He cut my hair short and shaved a small bald spot on the back of my head. My mother wouldn't let me go to school until the bald spot grew out again.

Of all my brothers and sisters (six in all), I am the only transplant to Athens, Ohio. I was born in Newark, Ohio, and have lived all around Southeastern Ohio. However, I moved to Athens to go to Ohio University and have never left.

At Ohio U, I never could make up my mind whether to major in English or Philosophy, so I got a bachelor's degree with a double major in both areas, then I added a Master of Arts degree in English and a Master of Arts degree in Philosophy. Yes, I have my MAMA degree.

Currently, and for a long time to come (I eat fruits and veggies), I am spending my retirement writing books such as *The Funniest People in Dance*, *Nadia Comaneci: Perfect 10*, *Homer's* Iliad: *A Retelling in Prose*, and *William Shakespeare's* Othello: *A Retelling in Prose*.

By the way, my sister Brenda Kennedy writes romances such as *A New Beginning* and *Shattered Dreams*.

Appendix C: Some Books by David Bruce

Anecdote Collections

250 Anecdotes About Opera
250 Anecdotes About Religion
250 Anecdotes About Religion: Volume 2
250 Music Anecdotes
Be a Work of Art: 250 Anecdotes and Stories
The Coolest People in Art: 250 Anecdotes
The Coolest People in the Arts: 250 Anecdotes
The Coolest People in Books: 250 Anecdotes
The Coolest People in Comedy: 250 Anecdotes
Create, Then Take a Break: 250 Anecdotes
Don't Fear the Reaper: 250 Anecdotes
The Funniest People in Art: 250 Anecdotes
The Funniest People in Books: 250 Anecdotes
The Funniest People in Books, Volume 2: 250 Anecdotes
The Funniest People in Books, Volume 3: 250 Anecdotes
The Funniest People in Comedy: 250 Anecdotes
The Funniest People in Dance: 250 Anecdotes
The Funniest People in Families: 250 Anecdotes
The Funniest People in Families, Volume 2: 250 Anecdotes
The Funniest People in Families, Volume 3: 250 Anecdotes
The Funniest People in Families, Volume 4: 250 Anecdotes
The Funniest People in Families, Volume 5: 250 Anecdotes
The Funniest People in Families, Volume 6: 250 Anecdotes
The Funniest People in Movies: 250 Anecdotes
The Funniest People in Music: 250 Anecdotes
The Funniest People in Music, Volume 2: 250 Anecdotes
The Funniest People in Music, Volume 3: 250 Anecdotes
The Funniest People in Neighborhoods: 250 Anecdotes
The Funniest People in Relationships: 250 Anecdotes
The Funniest People in Sports: 250 Anecdotes
The Funniest People in Sports, Volume 2: 250 Anecdotes
The Funniest People in Television and Radio: 250 Anecdotes
The Funniest People in Theater: 250 Anecdotes

The Funniest People Who Live Life: 250 Anecdotes
The Funniest People Who Live Life, Volume 2: 250 Anecdotes
The Kindest People Who Do Good Deeds, Volume 1: 250 Anecdotes
The Kindest People Who Do Good Deeds, Volume 2: 250 Anecdotes
Maximum Cool: 250 Anecdotes
The Most Interesting People in Movies: 250 Anecdotes
The Most Interesting People in Politics and History: 250 Anecdotes
The Most Interesting People in Politics and History, Volume 2: 250 Anecdotes
The Most Interesting People in Politics and History, Volume 3: 250 Anecdotes
The Most Interesting People in Religion: 250 Anecdotes
The Most Interesting People in Sports: 250 Anecdotes
The Most Interesting People Who Live Life: 250 Anecdotes
The Most Interesting People Who Live Life, Volume 2: 250 Anecdotes
Reality is Fabulous: 250 Anecdotes and Stories
Resist Psychic Death: 250 Anecdotes
Seize the Day: 250 Anecdotes and Stories

[1] Source: Doris G. Monteux, *It's All in the Music*, p. 102.

[2] Source: Herbert H. Breslin, editor, *The Tenors*, p. 123.

[3] Source: Mabel Wagnalls, *Stars of the Opera*, pp. 179-180.

[4] Source: Alfred Rossi, *Astonish Us in the Morning*, p. 149.

[5] Source: Mary Garden and Louis Biancolli, *Mary Garden's Story*, pp. 274-275.

[6] Source: Karl Böhm, *A Life Remembered: Memoirs*, p. 97.

[7] Source: Mabel Wagnalls, *Stars of the Opera*, p. 270.

[8] Source: Clara Kathleen Rogers (Clara Doria), *Memories of a Musical Career*, pp. 464-465.

[9] Source: Edwin McArthur, *Flagstad: A Personal Memoir*, p. 41.

[10] Source: David Ewen, *Listen to the Mocking Words*, p. 88.

[11] Source: Hugh Vickers, *Great Operatic Disasters*, p. 65.

[12] Source: Alan Wagner, *Prima Donnas and Other Wild Beasts*, p. 162.

[13] Source: Doris Jadan, *The Great Life of Ivan Jadan*, pp. 78-79.

[14] Source: Colonel J. H. Mapleson, *The Mapleson Memoirs*, p. 160.

[15] Source: Walter Slezak, *What Time's the Next Swan?*, p. 209.

[16] Source: Ted Cott, *The Victor Book of Musical Fun*, p. 93.

[17] Source: Hugh Vickers, *Great Operatic Disasters*, p. 40.

[18] Source: Art Linkletter, *I Wish I'd Said That!*, p. 63.

[19] Source: Sir Rudolf Bing, *A Knight at the Opera*, p. 23.

[20] Source: T.R. Ybarra, *Caruso: The Man of Naples and the Voice of God*, pp. 242-243.

[21] Source: Herbert H. Breslin, editor, *The Tenors*, pp. 19-20.

[22] Source: Barrymore Laurence Scherer, *Bravo! A Guide to Opera for the Perplexed*, pp. 243-244, 247.

[23] Source: *Pavarotti in Opera*, p. 33.

[24] Source: Penelope Turing, *Hans Hotter, Man and Artist*, p. 98.

[25] Source: Opera Magazine Ltd., *Tenors in Opera*, pp. 7-8.

[26] Source: Robert Lawrence, *A Rage for Opera*, p. 9.

[27] Source: Robert Lawrence, *A Rage for Opera*, pp. 5-6.

[28] Source: Henry C. Lahee, *Famous Singers of To-day and Yesterday*, pp. 66-67.

[29] Source: Patrick J. Smith, *A Year at the Met*, p. 206.

[30] Source: Henry Pleasants, *The Great Singers: From the Dawn of Opera to Our Own Time*, pp. 259-260.

[31] Source: Leslie Garrett, *Notes from a Small Soprano*, pp. 131-132.

[32] Source: Helen Traubel, *St. Louis Woman*, pp. 149-150.

[33] Source: Bridget Paolucci, *Beverly Sills*, p. 50.

[34] Source: Nancy Caldwell Sorel and Edward Sorel, *First Encounters*, p. 23.

[35] Source: Lanfranco Rasponi, *The Last Prima Donnas*, pp. 420-421.

[36] Source: Marilyn Horne, *Marilyn Horne: My Life*, p. 43.

[37] Source: Joshua Jampol, *Living Opera*, pp. 152-153.

[38] Source: Doris G. Monteux, *It's All in the Music*, p. 107.

[39] Source: Jack and Waltraud Karkar, compilers and editors, ... *And They Danced On*, p. 77.

[40] Source: David W. Barber, *If It Ain't Baroque...*, p. 103.

[41] Source: Mary Lawton, *Schumann-Heink: The Last of the Titans*, p. 234.

[42] Source: Toller Cranston, *Zero Tollerance*, p. 252.

[43] Source: Millicent Jones, *The World's Greatest Tenors*, pp. 31, 33-34.

[44] Source: Gretchen Finletter, *From the Top of the Stairs*, pp. 239-240.

[45] Source: Leo Slezak, *Song of Motley*, p. 127.

[46] Source: Helena Matheopoulos, *The Great Tenors From Caruso to the Present*, p. 76.

[47] Source: Geraldine Farrar, *Geraldine Farrar: The Story of an American Singer*, p. 12.

[48] Source: Andrea Bocelli, *The Music of Silence: A Memoir*, pp. 2-3.

[49] Source: Louisa Lauw, *Fourteen Years with Adelina Patti*, pp. 25-26.

[50] Source: Schuyler Chapin, *Sopranos, Mezzos, Tenors, Bassos, and Other Friends*, pp. 61-62.

[51] Source: Plácido Domingo, *My First Forty Years*, p. 73.

[52] Source: Evangelia Callas, *My Daughter Maria Callas*, p. 22.

[53] Source: Donald Brook, *Singers of Today*, pp. 167-168.

[54] Source: Sam Wellman, *Mariah Carey*, p. 16.

[55] Source: David L. Groover and Cecil C. Conner, Jr., *Skeletons from the Opera Closet*, p. 35.

[56] Source: Gretchen Finletter, *From the Top of the Stairs*, pp. 93-100, 147-148.

[57] Source: Bill Crow, *Jazz Anecdotes*, p. 54.

[58] Source: Salvatore Cortesi, *My Thirty Years of Friendships*, pp. 274-277.

[59] Source: Schuyler Chapin, *Sopranos, Mezzos, Tenors, Bassos, and Other Friends*, pp. 88-89.

[60] Source: Marjorie Lawrence, *Interrupted Melody: The Story of My Life*, p. 259.

[61] Source: Joan Hammond, *A Voice, A Life*, p. 118.

[62] Source: Joseph Benton, *Oklahoma Tenor: Musical Memories of Giuseppe Bentonelli*, pp. 113-114.

[63] Source: Helen L. Kaufmann, *Anecdotes of Music and Musicians*, pp. 240-241.

[64] Source: Barrymore Laurence Scherer, *Bravo! A Guide to Opera for the Perplexed*, p. 34.

[65] Source: Roland L. Bessette, *Mario Lanza: Tenor in Exile*, p. 63.

[66] Source: Nellie Melba, *Melodies and Memories*, pp. 102-104.

[67] Source: *Anton Seidl: A Memorial by His Friends*, pp. 62-63, 110-111.

[68] Source: Lotte Lehmann, *My Many Lives*, pp. 197-198.

[69] Source: Sir Georg Solti, "Foreword" to Penelope Turing, *Hans Hotter, Man and Artist*, pp. 13-14. Also, Penelope Turing, *Hans Hotter, Man and Artist*, p. 21.

[70] Source: Samuel Chotzinoff, *Toscanini: An Intimate Portrait*, pp. 44-45.

[71] Source: Karl Böhm, *A Life Remembered: Memoirs*, pp. 149-50.

[72] Source: Helen L. Kaufmann, *Anecdotes of Music and Musicians*, pp. 227-228.

[73] Source: Victor Borge and Robert Sherman, *My Favorite Comedies in Music*, p. 51.

[74] Source: David Ewen, *Famous Conductors*, p. 22.

[75] Source: Geraldine Farrar, *Such Sweet Compulsion*, p. 277.

[76] Source: Bridget Paolucci, *Beverly Sills*, p. 70.

[77] Source: David W. Barber, *When the Fat Lady Sings*, p. 131.

[78] Source: James A. Drake and Kristin Beall Ludecke, editors, *Lily Pons: A Centennial Portrait*, p. 9.

[79] Source: Rosalyn M. Story, *And So I Sing: African-American Divas of Opera and Concert*, p. 153.

[80] Source: Gerald Moore, *Am I Too Loud? Memoirs of an Accompanist*, pp. 76-77, 92-93, 107, 119.

[81] Source: Stephen E. Rubin, *The New Met in Profile*, pp. 68-69.

[82] Source: Donald Peck, *The Right Time, The Right Place! Tales of Chicago Symphony Days*, pp. 81-82.

[83] Source: Lily McCormack, *I Hear You Calling Me*, p. 127.

[84] Source: Clara Kathleen Rogers (Clara Doria), *Memories of a Musical Career*, p. 380.

[85] Source: Joshua Jampol, *Living Opera*, p. 205.

[86] Source: Richard Barthelemy, *Memories of Caruso*, p. 13.

[87] Source: Elisabeth Schwarzkopf, *On and Off the Record: A Memoir of Walter Legge*, p. 78.

[88] Source: Rita Hunter, *Wait Till the Sun Shines, Nellie*, pp. 71-72.

[89] Source: Art Linkletter, *I Wish I'd Said That!*, p. 53.

[90] Source: David W. Barber, *When the Fat Lady Sings*, p. 114.

[91] Source: Stuart A. Kallen, *Great Composers*, pp. 79-80.

[92] Source: Dorothy Caruso, *Enrico Caruso: His Life and Death*, p. 277.

[93] Source: Grace Moore, *You're Only Human Once*, pp. 111-113.

[94] Source: Marjorie Lawrence, *Interrupted Melody: The Story of My Life*, pp. 57-58.

[95] Source: Studs Terkel, "Foreword" to Danny Newman, *Tales of a Theatrical Guru*, p. xii.

[96] Source: Guerilla Girls, *Bitches, Bimbos and Ballbreakers: The Guerilla Girls' Illustrated Guide to Female Stereotypes*, p. 79.

[97] Source: Alan Blackwood, *The Performing World of the Singer*, p. 32.

[98] Source: Feodor Ivanovitch Chaliapine, *Pages From My Life: An Autobiography*, pp.134-135, 137-138.

[99] Source: Daniel J. Wakin, "Schuyler Chapin, Champion of Arts in New York, Dies at 86." *New York Times*. 7 March 2009 <http://www.nytimes.com/2009/03/08/arts/music/08chapin.html?_r=2&ref=obituaries>.

[100] Source: Edward Greenfield, *Joan Sutherland*, p. 10.

[101] Source: Rebecca Stefoff, *Plácido Domingo*, pp. 62-63.

[102] Source: Roland L. Bessette, *Mario Lanza: Tenor in Exile*, p. 65.

[103] Source: Anna Russell, *I'm Not Making This Up, You Know*, pp. 148-149.

[104] Source: Opera Magazine Ltd., *Tenors in Opera*, p. 20.

[105] Source: Jürgen Kesting, *Luciano Pavarotti: The Myth of the Tenor*, p. 24.

[106] Source: Charles O'Connell, *The Other Side of the Record*, pp. 149-150.

[107] Source: Andrea Bocelli, *The Music of Silence: A Memoir*, p. 187.

[108] Source: Neville Cardus, editor, *Kathleen Ferrier: A Memoir*, p. 91.

[109] Source: David Ewen, *Famous Conductors*, pp. 35-36.

[110] Source: Evangelia Callas, *My Daughter Maria Callas*, p. 18.

[111] Source: *Anton Seidl: A Memorial by His Friends*, pp. 113, 157.

[112] Source: Beverly Sills, *Bubbles: A Self-Portrait*, p. 139.

[113] Source: Scott Beach, *Musicdotes*, p. 56.

[114] Source: Henry T. Finck, *My Adventures in the Golden Age of Music*, pp. 120-123.

[115] Source: John Francis Marion, *Lucrezia Bori of the Metropolitan Opera*, pp. 76-78, 94-95.

[116] Source: Doris Jadan, *The Great Life of Ivan Jadan*, pp. 62-63.

[117] Source: Dorothy Caruso and Torrance Goddard, *Wings of Song: The Story of Caruso*, pp. 103-104.

[118] Source: Edward Wagenknecht, *Seven Daughters of the Theater*, p. 36.

[119] Source: Francis Rogers, *Some Famous Singers of the 19th Century*, pp. 10, 20.

[120] Source: Barry Hewlett-Davies, *A Night at the Opera*, p. 27.

[121] Source: Salvatore Cortesi, *My Thirty Years of Friendships*, pp. 288-290.

[122] Source: David L. Groover and Cecil C. Conner, Jr., *Skeletons from the Opera Closet*, pp. 157-158.

[123] Source: Mary Jane Matz, *Opera Stars in the Sun: Intimate Glimpses of Metropolitan Personalities*, p. 98.

[124] Source: Rosalyn M. Story, *And So I Sing: African-American Divas of Opera and Concert*, p. 110.

[125] Source: Stephen E. Rubin, *The New Met in Profile*, pp. 84-85.

[126] Source: Edwin McArthur, *Flagstad: A Personal Memoir*, p. 44.

[127] Source: Danny Newman, *Tales of a Theatrical Guru*, p. 127.

[128] Source: Leo Slezak, *Song of Motley*, p. 182.

[129] Source: Gordon T. Ledbetter, *The Great Irish Tenor*, p. 52, 145.

[130] Source: Candido Bonvicini, *The Tenor's Son: My Days With Pavarotti*, p. 93.

[131] Source: H. Goddard Owen, *A Recollection of Marcella Sembrich*, pp. 17, 55-57.

[132] Source: Neville Cardus, editor, *Kathleen Ferrier: A Memoir*, p. 92.

[133] Source: Doug Tischler, "Opera's Lesbian Divas." 20 April 2008 <http://www.afterellen.com/people/2008/4/patriciaracette_bethclayton>.

[134] Source: Elisabeth Schwarzkopf, *On and Off the Record: A Memoir of Walter Legge*, pp. 131, 133-134.

[135] Source: Alan Wagner, *Prima Donnas and Other Wild Beasts*, p. 156.

[136] Source: Helena Matheopoulos, *The Great Tenors From Caruso to the Present*, p. 68.

[137] Source: Plácido Domingo, *My First Forty Years*, pp. 36-37.

[138] Source: Francoise Hudry, *Hugues Cuenod: With a Nimble Voice*, p. 70.

[139] Source: Dorothy Caruso, *Enrico Caruso: His Life and Death*, p. 152.

[140] Source: Millicent Jones, *The World's Greatest Tenors*, pp. 34, 37.

[141] Source: James W. Morrissey, *Noted Men and Women*, pp. 115-116.

[142] Source: Kenneth Williams, *Acid Drops*, p. 18.

[143] Source: Leslie Ayre, *The Wit of Music*, p. 24.

[144] Source: Henry Pleasants, *The Great Singers: From the Dawn of Opera to Our Own Time*, p. 171.

[145] Source: John Boyden, collector, *Stick to the Music: Scores of Orchestral Tales*, p. 13.

[146] Source: Victor Borge, *My Favorite Intervals*, p. 132.

[147] Source: Henry Pleasants, editor, *The Great Tenor Tragedy*, p. 160.

[148] Source: Rebecca Stefoff, *Plácido Domingo*, p. 91.

[149] Source: Victor Seroff, *Renata Tebaldi: The Woman and the Diva*, p. 50.

[150] Source: Samuel Chotzinoff, *Toscanini: An Intimate Portrait*, p. 63.

[151] Source: Mary Lawton, *Schumann-Heink: The Last of the Titans*, pp. 272-273.

[152] Source: Feodor Ivanovitch Chaliapine, *Pages From My Life: An Autobiography*, p. 122.

[153] Source: Victor Seroff, *Renata Tebaldi: The Woman and the Diva*, pp. 157-158.

[154] Source: Victoria Horne Oakie, compiler and editor, *"Dear Jack,"* p. 102.

[155] Source: Donald Peck, *The Right Time, The Right Place! Tales of Chicago Symphony Days*, pp. 85-86.

[156] Source: Colonel J. H. Mapleson, *The Mapleson Memoirs*, pp. 162-163.

[157] Source: Nellie Melba, *Melodies and Memories*, pp. 257, 259-262.

[158] Source: Joseph Benton, *Oklahoma Tenor: Musical Memories of Giuseppe Bentonelli*, pp. 17-19.

[159] Source: Emma Calvé, *My Life*, pp. 32-33.

[160] Source: John Francis Marion, *Lucrezia Bori of the Metropolitan Opera*, pp. 64-65.

[161] Source: John Boyden, collector, *Stick to the Music: Scores of Orchestral Tales*, p. 106.

[162] Source: Hugh Vickers, *Even Greater Operatic Disasters*, pp. 13-14.

[163] Source: Nancy Shear, *The Three Tenors*, pp. 32, 40.

[164] Source: Rita Hunter, *Wait Till the Sun Shines, Nellie*, p. 202.

[165] Source: David Blum, *Quintet: Five Journeys Toward Musical Fulfillment*, pp. 180-181.

[166] Source: Frances Alda, *Men, Women, and Tenors*, p. 141.

[167] Source: Ted Cott, *The Victor Book of Musical Fun*, p. 31.

[168] Source: Emma Albani, *Forty Years of Song*, pp. 73-74.

[169] Source: Hugh Vickers, *Even Greater Operatic Disasters*, p. 44.

[170] Source: Victor Borge and Robert Sherman, *My Favorite Comedies in Music*, p. 52 Also: Warren Boroson, "Sir Georg Solti Story." *New Jersey Jewish Standard*. 28 January 2011 <http://w.jstandard.com/index.php/content/item/16942/>.

[171] Source: Rose Heylbut and Aime Gerber, *Backstage at the Opera*, p. 198.

[172] Source: Richard Temple Savage, *A Voice from the Pit*, p. 129.

[173] Source: Henry T. Finck, *My Adventures in the Golden Age of Music*, p. 176.

[174] Source: Walter Slezak, *What Time's the Next Swan?*, p. 210.

[175] Source: Donald J. Sobol, *Encyclopedia Brown's Book of Wacky Sports*, p. 89.

[176] Source: Sir Rudolf Bing, *5000 Nights at the Opera*, p. 333.

[177] Source: Geraldine Farrar, *Geraldine Farrar: The Story of an American Singer*, pp. 61-62.

[178] Source: Noel Ross-Russell, *There Will I Sing*, p. 112.

[179] Source: Edward Greenfield, *Joan Sutherland*, pp. 4, 35.

[180] Source: Robert Morley, *Robert Morley's Book of Bricks*, p. 65.

[181] Source: Dorothy Caruso and Torrance Goddard, *Wings of Song: The Story of Caruso*, pp. 36-37, 76-77.

[182] Source: Walter Damrosch, *My Musical Life*, pp. 134-136.

[183] Source: Rose Heylbut and Aime Gerber, *Backstage at the Opera*, p. 186.

[184] Source: Henry C. Lahee, *Famous Singers of To-day and Yesterday*, p. 69.

[185] Source: Nicolas Slonimsky, *Slonimsky's Book of Musical Anecdotes*, pp. 118-120.

[186] Source: T.R. Ybarra, *Caruso: The Man of Naples and the Voice of God*, p. 72.

[187] Source: Louisa Lauw, *Fourteen Years with Adelina Patti*, pp. 48-49.

[188] Source: Stephen Tanner, *Opera Antics and Anecdotes*, p. 159.

[189] Source: Mary Garden and Louis Biancolli, *Mary Garden's Story*, pp. 259-260.

[190] Source: David Ewen, *Listen to the Mocking Words*, pp. 68-69.

[191] Source: Lotte Lehmann, *My Many Lives*, p. 143.

[192] Source: Opera Magazine Ltd., *Sopranos in Opera: Profiles of Fifteen Great Sopranos*, p. 42.

[193] Source: Richard Huggett, *Supernatural on Stage*, p. 100.

[194] Source: Opera Magazine Ltd., *Sopranos in Opera: Profiles of Fifteen Great Sopranos*, pp. 13-14.

[195] Source: Jürgen Kesting, *Luciano Pavarotti: The Myth of the Tenor*, p. 20.

[196] Source: David Blum, *Quintet: Five Journeys Toward Musical Fulfillment*, p. 172.

[197] Source: Harry Rasky, *Stratas*, pp. 23-24.

[198] Source: Beverly Sills, *Bubbles: A Self-Portrait*, pp. 12, 91.

[199] Source: Nigel Douglas, *More Legendary Voices*, p. 250.

[200] Source: Emma Calvé, *My Life*, pp. 49-50.

[201] Source: Sarah Caldwell, *Challenges: A Memoir of My Life in Opera*, p. 73.

[202] Source: Nigel Douglas, *More Legendary Voices*, pp. 189-190.

[203] Source: Mary Jane Matz, *Opera Stars in the Sun: Intimate Glimpses of Metropolitan Personalities*, p. 41.

[204] Source: Marilyn Horne, *Marilyn Horne: My Life*, p. 171.

[205] Source: Geraldine Farrar, *Such Sweet Compulsion*, pp. 277-278.

[206] Source: Anna Russell, *I'm Not Making This Up, You Know*, p. 164.

[207] Source: Stephen Tanner, *Opera Antics and Anecdotes*, p. 111.

[208] Source: Leslie Ayre, *The Wit of Music*, pp. 88-89.

[209] Source: Francis Rogers, *Some Famous Singers of the 19th Century*, p. 54.

[210] Source: Helen Traubel, *St. Louis Woman*, pp. 125-126, 176.

[211] Source: Henry T. Finck, *Musical Laughs*, pp. 11-12.

[212] Source: H. Allen Smith, *The Compleat Practical Joker*, p. 67.

[213] Source: Sir Rudolf Bing, *5000 Nights at the Opera*, pp. 253-254.

[214] Source: Lawrence J. Epstein, *A Treasury of Jewish Anecdotes*, p. 177.

[215] Source: John L. Brecknock and John Kennedy Melling, *Scaling the High Cs: The Musical Life of Tenor John L. Brecknock*, pp. 23, 106.

[216] Source: Nicolas Slonimsky, *Slonimsky's Book of Musical Anecdotes*, p. 148.

[217] Source: Nigel Douglas, *Legendary Voices*, pp. 233-234.

[218] Source: Walter Damrosch, *My Musical Life*, pp. 140-141.

[219] Source: Charles O'Connell, *The Other Side of the Record*, p. 88.

[220] Source: Barry Hewlett-Davies, *A Night at the Opera*, pp. 22-23.

[221] Source: James A. Drake and Kristin Beall Ludecke, editors, *Lily Pons: A Centennial Portrait*, p. 105.

[222] Source: Lanfranco Rasponi, *The Last Prima Donnas*, p. 420.

[223] Source: Emma Albani, *Forty Years of Song*, pp. 225-226.

[224] Source: Sir Rudolf Bing, *A Knight at the Opera*, p. 16.

[225] Source: Lily McCormack, *I Hear You Calling Me*, pp. 11-12, 74.

[226] Source: Leslie Garrett, *Notes from a Small Soprano*, p. 192.

[227] Source: Francoise Hudry, *Hugues Cuenod: With a Nimble Voice*, p. 68.

[228] Source: Mary Ellis Peltz, *The Magic of the Opera*, p. 31.

[229] Source: Henry T. Finck, *Musical Laughs*, p. 223.

[230] Source: Nigel Douglas, *Legendary Voices*, pp. 167-168.

[231] Source: Joan Hammond, *A Voice, A Life*, pp. 29-30.

[232] Source: David W. Barber, *If It Ain't Baroque...*, pp. 101-102.

[233] Source: Alan Blackwood, *The Performing World of the Singer*, p. 33.

[234] Source: Frances Alda, *Men, Women, and Tenors*, p. 20.

[235] Source: Harold Atkins and Archie Newman, *Beecham Stories*, pp. 37-38.

[236] Source: Candido Bonvicini, *The Tenor's Son: My Days With Pavarotti*, p. 18.

[237] Source: Nancy Shear, *The Three Tenors*, p. 60.

[238] Source: Richard Barthelemy, *Memories of Caruso*, p. 6.

[239] Source: John L. Brecknock and John Kennedy Melling, *Scaling the High Cs: The Musical Life of Tenor John L. Brecknock*, p. 44.

[240] Source: *Pavarotti in Opera*, p. 46.

[241] Source: "Obituary: Luciano Pavarotti." *The Guardian*. 7 September 2007 <http://music.guardian.co.uk/classical/operalivereviews/story/0,,2164060,00.html>.

[242] Source: Leonard Feather and Jack Tracy, *Laughter from the Hip: The Lighter Side of Jazz*, p. 170.

[243] Source: Sarah Caldwell, *Challenges: A Memoir of My Life in Opera*, pp. 91, 97-99.

[244] Source: Stuart A. Kallen, *Great Composers*, pp. 31, 33-34.

[245] Source: Richard Temple Savage, *A Voice from the Pit*, pp. 95-96.

[246] Source: Grace Moore, *You're Only Human Once*, pp. 32-33.

[247] Source: Henny Youngman, *Take My Life, Please!*, p. 29.

[248] Source: Paul Arendt, interviewer, "It was all about the voice." *The Guardian*. 7 September 2007 <http://music.guardian.co.uk/classical/story/0,,2164213,00.html>.

[249] Source: Donald Brook, *Singers of Today*, p. 153.

[250] Source: Patrick J. Smith, *A Year at the Met*, pp. 178-179.